Christ's Truth Over Heresy
by Richard Allen
with chapters by C. Matthew McMahon

Copyright Information

Christ's Truth Over Heresy, by Richard Allen, with chapters by C. Matthew McMahon
Edited by Therese B. McMahon

© 2025 by Puritan Publications and A Puritan's Mind

Published by Puritan Publications
A Ministry of A Puritan's Mind®
Crossville, TN: Puritan Publications, 2025
www.puritanpublications.com
www.apuritansmind.com
www.gracechapeltn.com
www.reformedsynod.com

All rights reserved. No part of this publication may be reproduced, stored in a retrieval system or transmitted in any form by any means, electronic, mechanical, photocopy, recording or otherwise, without the prior permission of the publisher, except as provided by USA copyright law.

First Electronic Edition 2025
First Modern Print Edition 2025
Manufactured in the United States of America

eISBN: 978-1-62663-512-8
ISBN: 978-1-62663-513-5

Table of Contents

Meet Richard Allen 5

A Theological Defense of Truth 11

To the Reader 19

The Preface 22

Chapter 1: Of the Holy Scriptures 26

Chapter 2: Of the Blessed Trinity 36

Chapter 3: Of the Creation 49

Chapter 4: Of Divine Providence 53

Chapter 5: Of the Fall of Man, and of Original sin ... 58

Chapter 6: Of Freewill 63

Chapter 7: Of Christ's Person 67

Chapter 8: Of Christ's Office 71

Chapter 9: The Death of Christ 74

Chapter 10: The Resurrection of Christ 78

Chapter 11: Of Predestination 81

Chapter 12: Of Vocation 87

Chapter 13: Of Justification 92

Chapter 14: Of Sanctification 96

Chapter 15: Of the Moral Law 100

Chapter 16: Of Good Works 103

Chapter 17: Of Death and Burial 107

Chapter 18: Of the Resurrection 111

Chapter 19: Of Glorification in Heaven 113

Chapter 20: Of Hell 115

Chapter 21: Of Purgatory 118

Chapter 22: Of Images 121

Chapter 23: Of the Church 124

Chapter 24: Of the Sacraments 132

Chapter 25: Of Baptism..136

Chapter 26: Of the Lord's Supper............................... 140

Chapter 27: Of Reformation..147

Chapter 28: Of Toleration 154

A Gainful Death: The End of a Truly Christian Life 156

Other Books on Heresy at Puritan Publications 180

Meet Richard Allen
by C. Matthew McMahon, Ph.D., Th.D.

Richard Allen (baptized in 1604) was a devoted Puritan minister known for his unwavering commitment to his faith and his refusal to conform to ecclesiastical mandates that conflicted with his conscience. His life, marked by trials and persecutions, exemplifies the resilience of many nonconforming ministers of his era.

Early Life and Ministry

Allen served as the minister at Ednam in Lincolnshire. Described as a "good preacher" who was "much beloved." His ministry before Christ was distinguished by his theological integrity and dedication to his congregation. However, his nonconformity to the Church of England's requirements led to significant hardships. In 1583, following the publication of Archbishop Whitgift's *Three Articles*, Allen was suspended from his ministerial duties for refusing to subscribe to the imposed regulations.

Whitgift's *Three Articles* sought to enforce uniformity within the Church by requiring ministers to swear absolute adherence to the *Thirty-Nine Articles*, acknowledge the *Book of Common Prayer*, and uphold the *Queen's* supremacy. While Allen and many others willingly subscribed to the first and third articles, which affirmed royal authority and the general articles of faith, they could not in good conscience affirm the second article related to the *entirety* of the Common Prayer. This refusal led to their suspension from ministry.[1]

The Supplication to the Lords of the Council

Following their suspension, Allen and twenty fellow ministers from Lincolnshire presented a formal supplication to the Lords of the Council. Their plea highlighted the spiritual plight of their congregations, who were deprived of pastoral care due to their refusal to comply with the ecclesiastical demands. In their supplication, they wrote:

> "For as much, right honourable, as we whose names are underwritten, whom the Lord in rich mercy hath placed over some of his people in Lincolnshire, as pastors to feed them with the word of truth, do humbly beseech your honours to regard the pitiful and woeful state of our congregations in those parts; which being destitute of our ministry, by means of the subscription now generally and strictly urged by the bishops, do mourn and lament."

The ministers emphasized that their refusal was not out of arrogance but due to unresolved doubts about several *practices* (those violating the Regulative Principle) in the Book of Common Prayer. Their primary concern was

---

[1] MS. *Register*, p. 331.

maintaining peace of conscience while fulfilling their spiritual duties to Christ the King. The petition concludes with an earnest appeal for restoration to their flocks so they could "go forwards in the Lord's work".[2]

Persecution and Restoration

Although the outcome of their supplication remains unclear, it is known that Allen was eventually restored to his ministerial role. He later served as a preacher at Louth in Lincolnshire. However, his troubles resurfaced in 1596 when Judge Anderson targeted him for further persecution. Anderson's disdain for nonconforming ministers was notorious, and he pursued Puritans with a relentless zeal.

Allen's indictment stemmed from his omission of certain prayers during services to allow more time for his sermons. This omission led to his being summoned to the assizes, where he was publicly humiliated. Anderson, adopting a fierce demeanor, accused Allen of grievous crimes without specifying any particular offense. Throughout the proceedings, Anderson repeatedly called him a "knave" and a "rebellious knave," depriving Allen of the opportunity to defend himself.

Despite this harsh treatment, Allen displayed remarkable humility and patience. He refrained from retaliating, demonstrating the Puritan commitment to meekness under persecution. When a theological

---

[2] Ibid.

question arose during the trial, Allen deferred to the bishop present for clarification. However, Anderson's fury only intensified. He rebuked Allen, declaring, "I am your ordinary and bishop too, in this place," and dared anyone to challenge his authority.

A Wider Pattern of Injustice

The treatment of Richard Allen exemplifies the broader pattern of persecution faced by Puritan ministers in Elizabethan and early Stuart England. These ministers were often portrayed as seditious troublemakers, equated with criminals, and subjected to public scorn. Judge Anderson's animosity towards Allen reflects the extent to which Puritans were vilified. Sir George Sampol's quiet defense of Allen, noting his honest character and godly conduct, did little to sway the judge's wrath.

The trial highlights the systemic challenges Puritan ministers faced in their pursuit of spiritual reform. Despite their theological orthodoxy and loyalty to the Crown, their refusal to conform to ecclesiastical ceremonies led to their being marginalized and criminalized. Allen's experience underscores the Puritan belief that fidelity to God's Word outweighed allegiance to human mandates.

Later Life and Legacy

While records do not specify the immediate outcome of Allen's prosecution, his story aligns with the enduring legacy of Puritan nonconformity. His steadfastness in the face of oppression serves as a testament to his faith and his commitment to *pastoral care*. Allen's trials reflect the broader struggle of Puritan ministers who sought to uphold scriptural purity while navigating the treacherous waters of ecclesiastical authority.

Allen's personal life also offers insight into his character. Born in Warminster, Wiltshire, possibly around 1602, he was the son of William Allen.[3] He married Priscilla Mullins in 1626 in Keynsham, Somerset, and they had several children, including Samuel Allen, John Allen, Nathaniel Allen, Priscilla Allen, and Thomas Allen. Allen may have died on August 10 (1651-52?), and buried at St. John's Church in Keynsham.[4] His will was proven on January 30, 1652, provides further evidence of his family's status and his enduring legacy.

Richard Allen's life embodies the tensions that characterized Puritan ministry in early modern England. His resistance to conformity was not born of rebellion but of a conscientious commitment to *biblical truth* and the sovereign reign of King Jesus. Despite the disdain of figures like Judge Anderson, Allen remained a model of humility and perseverance. His legacy as a preacher, husband, and father endures as a reminder of the

---

[3] *Warminster Records*, St. Denys, 1566-1894.
[4] *Keynsham St. John's Burials*, 1628-1684.

spiritual convictions that shaped the Puritan movement and the sacrifices made in pursuit of faithful ministry. His life serves as a wonderful example of how faithfulness to God's Word can endure despite the harshest adversities.

Allen's story, though only a fragment of the broader Puritan struggle, sheds light on the importance of religious liberty and the courage required to uphold truth in the face of injustice. The memory of his faithfulness continues to inspire those who seek to serve with integrity and courage.

Further Sources:
- *Warminster Records*, St. Denys, 1566-1894
- *Keynsham St. John's Burials*, 1628-1684
- *Abstracts of Probate Acts in the Prerogative Court of Canterbury*, Church of England, Province of Canterbury
- *MS. Register*

A Theological Defense of Truth
by C. Matthew McMahon, Ph.D., Th.D.

If there's one thing that becomes clear as you make your way through Richard Allen's writings, it's that this is no mere academic treatise, nor is it a pamphlet of pleasantries to comfort the religiously fainthearted. No, Allen's work is a trumpet blast in an age riddled with confusion, compromise, and outright heresy (yes, that's our day today in the life of the contemporary "evangelical" church). His book stands as a defiant declaration of what it *means* to be the true Church, to be a true Christian, to walk in obedience to Christ, and to anchor oneself firmly in biblical truth amid a tempest of competing doctrines.

Allen's work unfolds like a theological fortress. Every chapter is another stone laid upon the foundation of Scripture, fortified with historical and doctrinal insights, all with the aim of defending the purity of the Church and the necessity of Christ's unshakable authority over her. At its heart, this book is a defense of the Gospel against the tides of error that seek to erode its beauty and power. Here, Allen addresses the wonderful use of the *Solemn League and Covenant* as it pertains to the role of theology in the Church, the use of sacraments, how godly reformation occurs, worship and the limits of religious toleration—all while pointing the reader back to the cross and the blood of Christ as the unbreakable center of the Christian life.

Theological Defense

The history of Christ's Church is marked by seasons of doctrinal purity and seasons of theological corruption. The latter arise when heresy spreads under the guise of new insights, misguided tolerance, or the influence of worldly philosophies creeping into sacred doctrine. Allen's *antidote* is not merely a polemic against error but a wake-up call to the Church to remain steadfast in the faith once delivered to the saints (Jude 1:3). In an age where the purity of the Gospel was constantly assailed, Allen undertook the solemn task of contending for biblical truth, exposing the subtle and destructive nature of doctrinal deviations.

This work is more than an intellectual engagement with heresy—it is a theological fortress erected to preserve the integrity of Christian doctrine. Allen systematically refutes the principal heresies of his time, from distortions of the Trinity to corruptions of justification, sanctification, and the nature of the Church. He does not approach these matters with a cold, detached analysis but with the urgency of a shepherd guarding the flock against wolves.

At the heart of Allen's argument is an unwavering commitment to *sola Scriptura*—the authority of God's Word as the final standard for faith and practice. He meticulously demonstrates how heretical movements often elevate human reason, tradition, or mystical experience above the clear teaching of Scripture. From Rome's additions to the Gospel to the radical sects that sought to undermine it altogether,

Allen traces how deviations from biblical orthodoxy inevitably lead to spiritual ruin.

Yet, this book is not merely a warning; it is also an encouragement to those who love Christ's truth. Allen's work reminds us that theological vigilance is not an option but a *necessity*. The purity of the Church is not maintained through passive indifference but through active discernment and a firm adherence to the unchanging truth of God's Word.

In an era where theological compromise is often mistaken for charity and doctrinal precision is dismissed as divisiveness, his work stands as a *timeless* reminder that truth must never be sacrificed on the altar of human opinion. Allen's words remain as relevant today as when they were first penned, urging us to hold fast to the faith, resist error, and glorify Christ as the sole and sovereign Head of His Church.

A Theology for the Church and About the Church

Allen strips away any illusions about what the theology of the Church is and isn't. He contends that the true Church is not merely a building adorned with ornaments or a mixed multitude of nominal believers and hypocrites. The true Church, he asserts, is the company of God's elect—those redeemed by Christ's blood and called into fellowship with Him. It is invisible in the sense that only God knows its full number, and yet it is visible in its *public profession*, its ordinances, and

Theological Defense

its witness to the world. This work is about its public confession.

For Allen, the Church's identity is tied directly to its fidelity to Christ as its head as it understands him and understands itself. Any deviation—whether by indulgence in superstition, corruption of leadership, or compromise in doctrine—is a grievous *betrayal*. He warns against the dangers of idolatry, particularly as seen in the Roman Church's abuses, where altars replaced tables, crucifixes replaced pure worship, and the Pope replaced Christ as the supposed head of the Church.

The Sacraments: Signs, Seals, and Sacred Responsibility

Allen's treatment of the church and sacraments is both pastoral and polemical. He anchors his argument in the fact that the sacraments—Baptism and the Lord's Supper—are not empty rituals but holy ordinances instituted by Christ. Baptism is described as the sign of admission into the covenant community, not as a means of regeneration but as a declaration of the work of grace already wrought by the Holy Spirit. Infant baptism, in particular, is fiercely defended as consistent with the covenantal promises of God.

Regarding the Lord's Supper, Allen takes aim at the errors of Transubstantiation and Consubstantiation, refuting the notion that the bread and wine become or contain the literal body and blood of Christ. Instead, he asserts the spiritual presence of Christ in the sacrament—real and true, though not physical. The Lord's Supper, for Allen, is a sacred moment of communion with Christ, a strengthening of faith, and a foretaste of the heavenly banquet yet to come.

Reformation and the Church's Need for Purity

Allen is unflinching in his call for theological reformation. He reminds his readers that no church, no matter how esteemed, is immune to corruption. Like a building that requires regular repairs, the Church must continually be *reformed* according to Scripture. Allen condemns the superficial, ceremonial trappings that had crept into worship, such as altars disguised as tables and the bowing rituals associated with them. To him, these are not mere matters of preference but dangerous deviations that threaten to dilute the pure worship of God.

Yet, Allen does not call for a destructive reformation that tears down everything for the sake of novelty. Instead, he calls for a *restoration*—a return to the simplicity and purity of the Church as it was established by Christ and His apostles. His words are a rebuke to both those who tolerate sin for the sake of peace and those who sow discord for the sake of so-called purity.

The Question of Toleration: No Room for Error

In his era where calls for religious toleration were gaining momentum, Allen stands firmly against the idea of allowing error to flourish under the guise of liberty. For Allen, theological error is not a harmless weed to be left alone—it is a *cancer* that, if left unchecked, will spread and corrupt the whole body. He cites the Apostle Paul's refusal to give false teachers even an hour's platform (Galatians 1:5) as a model for the Church. The purity of the Gospel is too precious to be sacrificed on the altar of inclusivity.

Allen's view may strike modern ears as severe, but his concern is pastoral at its core. He understood that, to tolerate doctrinal error was to jeopardize the souls of the flock. His warnings against sectarianism, heresy, and spiritual apathy are as relevant now as they were in his time.

The Unwavering Hope: Underneath the Blood of Christ

Throughout his work, Allen's ultimate focus is clear: the sufficiency of Christ's atonement and the believer's security under His blood. The Christian life, with all its trials and triumphs, is lived beneath the shadow of the cross. Every chapter pulses with the reminder that Christ's sacrifice is the foundation of *all* hope, joy, and perseverance.

Allen's emphasis on the reformational power of Christ's blood speaks directly to the believer's need for assurance. In a fallen world filled with temptation, persecution, and the fear of death, he anchors his readers in the truth that to live is Christ, and to die is gain. The Church may be assaulted, doctrines may be challenged, and Christians may stumble, but the blood of Christ remains a sure and steadfast refuge to guide the believer into "all truth."

Also Included: "A Gainful Death"

The appended funeral sermon, *A Gainful Death: The End of a Truly Christian Life*, serves as a fitting conclusion to Allen's work. Preached at the funeral of Mr. John Griffith, this sermon is a heartfelt meditation on the Christian's *victory* over death. Allen reflects on the Apostle Paul's declaration, "To live is Christ, and to die is gain," (Philippians 1:21) and unpacks the glorious truth that death is not a defeat but a promotion to eternal life.

In the sermon, Allen reminds his listeners that the Christian's gain by death includes freedom from sin, suffering, and sorrow, as well as entrance into the immediate presence of Christ. He emphasizes the believer's union with Christ as the key to facing death without fear. With vivid language and pastoral warmth, Allen calls his audience to examine their lives, in light of eternity, and to find comfort in the hope of the resurrection.

Overall, Richard Allen's work is not for the faint-hearted or the lukewarm. It is a bold and unwavering defense of biblical orthodoxy, a call to worship God in spirit and truth, and an exhortation to stand firm in the faith once delivered to the saints. For the reader willing to engage with its depth and gravity, this book offers not only theological instruction but spiritual fortification.

May this introduction serve as a reminder of the treasure that lies within these pages and stir you to consider, as Allen would have you do, whether Christ is indeed *your life* and whether His truth is important to you. For if He is, and if the truth of the Gospel is important, then even in the darkest valleys of this life, you can proclaim with confidence that the Bible is true, and you can know what God has taught in it, so that your life of holiness would shine and reflect His glory.

In Christ's grace and mercy,
C. Matthew McMahon, Ph.D., Th.D.
From My study, February, 2025
"...search the Scriptures..." (John 5:39).
www.apuritansmind.com
www.puritanpublications.com
www.gracechapeltn.com
www.reformedsynod.com

To the Reader

To the Right Honorable the Lord's and Commons Assembled in Parliament

Grace and peace be multiplied.

Right Honorable,

Divisions in the Church have always led to divisions within the nation, and divisions in the nation typically deepen the divisions within the Church. Differences in religion were the root cause of these tragic and unnatural wars; and instead of resolving them, these wars have only intensified such divisions. Despite the *Solemn League and Covenant* to eradicate all forms of Popery, heresy, and schism, as well as your recent, godly ordinance aimed at curbing the spread of these errors, and despite the dedicated work of many learned men, heresies have multiplied beyond count. Like uncontrolled waters, the more they are restrained, the more fiercely they rise and swell.

Indeed, heresy, profaneness, barbarism, and atheism have always accompanied war as closely as famine and pestilence. Times of war and chaos provide ample opportunity for the adversary to sow his tares, just as times of peace, sleep, and complacency do. To address these divisions, the Italians have a proverb: "Hard to hard never makes a good stone wall." They mean that in any conflict, some measure of yielding is necessary for unity to be established.

In matters of religion, I have dared to do something—my calling compels me to act—with an intense longing to see peace and truth firmly established among us. I humbly present these small labors to your Honors, hoping you will receive them with goodwill, recognizing that while they may fall short of their intended goal, they are offered in service of that good purpose. Accept this humble work, for even the smallest stone helps to repair the largest breach.

When I heard the most horrendous blasphemies and saw the monstrous heresies that sprang up daily—bringing dishonor to Almighty God, reproach to His truth, and grief to the hearts of His people—while the enemy seemed to triumph and trample everything underfoot, I set aside my doubts and fears and completed this small book. I was moved to do so not only to make use of my recent unwelcome leisure but, more importantly, to fulfill my duty in two specific ways:

1. As a Christian: For we are all bound by the apostle's exhortation, "...earnestly contend for the faith which was once delivered unto the saints," (Jude 1:3).

2. As a minister of the Gospel of Jesus Christ: It is our special charge to defend the truth and to resist false teachers steadfastly, "...no, not for an hour; that the truth of the gospel might continue with you," (Galatians 2:5).

Additionally, the *Solemn Covenant* obliges us to root out all heresy, schism, profaneness, and whatever contradicts sound doctrine.

Now, I humbly present this work to you as it is. I was further encouraged to do so by the many favors and kindnesses I have received from you. Please accept this book as a token of my gratitude.

I pray that it may serve as a helpful guide to expose the many deceptions and schemes of false prophets and deceivers who have entered the world, introducing destructive heresies and even denying the Lord who redeemed them. Many follow their destructive ways, yet my constant prayer is that you may always escape their snares.

Your most obliged nephew,
Your Honors' humble servant,
RICHARD ALLEN

The Preface

God has never performed a miracle solely to prove His existence to atheists because His ordinary works provide sufficient evidence. As it is written, *"For the invisible things of him from the creation of the world are clearly seen, being understood by the things that are made, even his eternal power and Godhead; so that they are without excuse,"* (Romans 1:20). No nation has ever been found so barbaric as to deny the existence of a god altogether. Even the most uncivilized societies professed some form of religion. Human nature itself recoils from outright atheism so strongly that the heathen preferred making gods of wood and stone rather than having no gods at all. They bestowed divine honors not only upon men like themselves but even upon base and vile creatures rather than be without religion altogether.

Since the devil could not uproot the belief in a divine being, which is deeply embedded in the hearts of all people by nature, he redirected his efforts from atheism to heathenism. Rather than deny the divine altogether, he promoted the multiplication of deities. With countless false gods, he deluded the world for nearly four thousand years.

When the fullness of time had come, God sent His Son as a light to the Gentiles. The brilliance of Christ's truth dispelled the fog of paganism. The deceptions of idolatry were exposed, and consciences were convicted of their former ignorance. Many turned from dead idols to serve the living God. However, the old serpent adapted his tactics yet again. Cast out from the stronghold of heathenism, he turned to *heresy*. Instead of introducing false gods, he set up *false* worship of the true God. In this, he multiplied his corruptions so extensively that there are now as many false worship practices as there once were false gods.

To trace this deceitful serpent through his many twists and turns *from the early Church* to the present and to observe the subtle methods he has used to infiltrate the very heart of the Church, poisoning its members and distorting every point of doctrine, is a task far too vast for this small volume. Nevertheless, a brief summary may provide some illumination.

The first person the devil used to spread heresy in the New Testament was Simon Magus, as recorded in Acts 8. He bewitched the people of Samaria, earning the title of "the father of all heretics." His heresy became the cursed womb from which an entire brood of heresies was born, covering the earth and establishing a mighty kingdom for the devil.

Today, that kingdom is divided into two main provinces. In the East, there is the Mohammedan sect, led by the Turk as its viceroy. In the West, there is the Antichristian faction, led by the Pope as its vicar. Under these two generals, the enemies of Christ are enlisted—both those who oppose His person and those who oppose His office. Though they may seem to differ outwardly, they share a hidden alliance. Like Samson's foxes, their heads point in different directions, but their tails are tied together. These are the foxes that spoil the Lord's vineyard, causing more harm through deceit than wild boars do through open destruction.

Balaam, the false prophet, caused more damage to the Israelites through his treachery than the Amorites with all their armies. Likewise, the heretic Arius caused more harm to the Christian Church than the savage emperors did with all their legions.

It is no wonder, then, that Scripture *repeatedly* warns us to beware of seducers and false teachers. As it is written, *"For there are certain men crept in unawares,"* (Jude 1:4). These false teachers introduce their heresies *secretly* and deceive others with feigned words (2 Peter 2:1, 3). They have an outward appearance of godliness (2 Timothy 3:5), using their polished exteriors to gain entrance into our hearts, where they ensnare and lead believers into captivity.

We must be vigilant, for these deceivers grow worse and worse, both deceiving others and being deceived themselves (2 Timothy 3:13). They travel across sea and land, filling both towns and countrysides. Not only do they creep into houses, but they also ascend to positions of influence, growing bolder in their efforts.

Just as Jannes and Jambres withstood Moses, these men resist the truth. They are of corrupt minds and lack sound judgment concerning *the faith* (2 Timothy 3:8). To prevent them from advancing further, their errors must be exposed so that they may be recognized and avoided.

Though it is impossible to uncover every heresy within the scope of this work, I have endeavored to highlight the principal errors, which serve as the *root* of many others. The purpose of this small book is to equip those who are weaker in the faith with general answers from God's Word to counter the arguments of the adversaries. While these answers may not be enough to defeat the enemy entirely, I hope they will be sufficient for self-defense so that believers will be prepared whenever they encounter false teachings and will not be caught off guard and led astray by the error of the wicked (2 Peter 3:17).

These efforts represent the first fruits of a larger endeavor. If this small offering is accepted, it is but a handful taken from a much larger harvest.

RICHARD ALLEN

Imprimatur:
James Cranford, March 28, 1648.

Chapter 1:
Of the Holy Scriptures

The Authority of the Holy Scriptures.

 The Holy Scriptures of the Old and New Testaments are the very Word of God, written by holy men as they were moved by the Holy Spirit. These Scriptures contain everything necessary for knowledge and belief leading to eternal salvation and are fully sufficient to instruct the Church of God in all matters of faith and practice. By "holy Scripture," we refer only to those books that have been historically recognized and are now accepted by the Church of England as canonical.

Errors Opposing the Authority of Scripture
 There are many adversaries who challenge this truth, but their errors can generally be categorized into three groups:
1. Those who add to the canon of Scripture, introducing elements that do not belong.
2. Those who diminish the canon, denying certain parts and removing some books.
3. Those who reject the entirety of Scripture, dismissing its divine authority and viewing it as mere human writings.

 1. Those Who Reject Scripture Entirely. In the early Church, figures such as Simon Magus and Montanus

were known for rejecting the authority of the Scriptures. In more recent times, this error is perpetuated by certain Anabaptists, who refer to the written Word as a "dead letter" and base their doctrines on personal revelations, dreams, and visions. They give such credence to these supposed revelations that, in Sangal, a town in Switzerland, one of them murdered his brother, claiming he had received a divine command to do so.[5]

This same method was used by Mohammed, who attributed his *epileptic seizures* to divine trances in which he claimed to receive revelations from heaven. Similarly, false prophets like Muncer, Becold, and Cnipperdolling in Germany led many miserable souls to destruction under the guise of divine revelation.

The Papists also diminish the authority of Scripture by asserting that the Scriptures are no more trustworthy than mere fables unless sanctioned by the Church. They remove the Scriptures from the hands of laypeople, claiming that reading them is dangerous, and have even burned Bibles and men alike for possessing the Scriptures in a known language.

2. Those Who Diminish the Canon. Some adversaries do not reject the entire body of Scripture but diminish its authority by denying certain portions:

1. The Jews reject the entire New Testament.
2. The Libertines claim that the Old Testament is abolished.

---

[5] Sleidan, *Commentaries*, Book 6.

3. The Socinians argue that the Old Testament is unnecessary and dispensable.

3. Those Who Add to the Canon. Others attempt to enlarge the canon of Scripture by adding elements that do not belong. The Papists are guilty of this, introducing traditions—unwritten so-called "truths"—and fables as necessary supplements to Scripture. They claim that the Scriptures are incomplete and require the addition of apocryphal books, traditions, and human inventions to provide a complete guide to salvation.

The Scriptures as the Touchstone of Truth

The Scriptures are the only reliable standard by which truth and error can be discerned. They are called a testament because they bear witness to God's most holy will. Against all adversaries and their errors, we firmly assert:

1. **The Scriptures of the Old and New Testaments are the very Word of God.** They possess sufficient authority without the endorsement of the Church or any human testimony to establish doctrine and settle religious controversies.

Just as the authority of a writing depends on the authority of its author, so the Scriptures, authored by God, possess divine authority and are inherently trustworthy.

Evidence for the Divine Authority of Scripture

First, the authors of Scripture were called and sent by God. These men were empowered by God and confirmed their teachings with signs and wonders beyond human ability. Though they were simple and unlearned, they wrote of profound divine mysteries that transcend human understanding and captivate even the angels (1 Peter 1:12).

Second, the doctrine contained in Scripture is divine and true. The Scriptures convey heavenly truths and have proven accurate in every prophecy and foretelling. Despite being written across different times, places, and by various authors on diverse topics, all the books of Scripture harmonize beautifully as though they were dictated by one and the same Spirit of truth.

Third, the effects of Scripture are unparalleled. No other writings have produced such remarkable transformations. Though its teachings often contradict human reason and challenge natural desires, Scripture has the power to win hearts and change lives. It discerns thoughts, comforts the soul, enlightens the mind, convicts the conscience, and renews the entire person, conforming them to the image of God in true holiness.

Fourth, the Scriptures have triumphed over the world. Despite being proclaimed by weak and humble men, the Word of God has brought mighty nations into submission to Christ, overcoming fierce opposition. The preservation of Scripture is itself a miracle, as countless efforts have been made to destroy

Chapter 1: Of the Holy Scriptures

it. Yet, the Word of God endures, undiminished and indestructible.

The Scriptures remain the true and unshakable witness of God's will, standing firm against every attempt to corrupt or diminish their authority.

Fifthly, the testimony of the Church, when considered rightly, is a significant support for faith. The unified confession of Christians across all ages, especially the sufferings of holy martyrs who defended the Scriptures at the cost of their lives, lends further credibility to their divine origin.

Sixthly, the testimony of the Holy Spirit to our hearts and consciences removes all doubt. The Spirit not only persuades but fully assures us that the Scriptures are the Word of God. This is referred to as the sealing of the Spirit, as it is written, *"In whom ye also trusted, after that ye heard the word of truth, the gospel of your salvation: in whom also after that ye believed, ye were sealed with that holy Spirit of promise,"* (Ephesians 1:13).

Lastly, the Scriptures testify of their own divine nature. As it is written, *"All Scripture is given by inspiration of God,"* (2 Timothy 3:16) and *"For the prophecy came not in old time by the will of man: but holy men of God spake as they were moved by the Holy Ghost,"* (2 Peter 1:21). The prophets always declared their messages with the authority of, "Thus saith the Lord" or "The mouth of the Lord hath spoken it."

The Scriptures, therefore, hold supreme and sovereign authority, surpassing that of the Church.

Their authority is as much greater than the Church's as God's authority is greater than man's. The Scriptures existed before the Church and are the immortal seed from which the Church grew. They are the foundation upon which the Church stands and the pillar that supports it, as it is written, *"And are built upon the foundation of the apostles and prophets, Jesus Christ himself being the chief corner stone,"* (Ephesians 2:20).

Irenaeus writes, "The authority of Him who spoke it is sufficient to confirm it."[6] Theodoritus affirms in his commentary on Ezekiel, "The Scriptures are to be the judge in all matters of controversy." As the prophet Isaiah declared, "To the law and to the testimony: if they speak not according to this word, it is because there is no light in them," (Isaiah 8:20). Christ Himself said, "Search the scriptures; for in them ye think ye have eternal life: and they are they which testify of me," (John 5:39). The Bereans "searched the scriptures daily, whether those things were so," (Acts 17:11).

Secondly, the Old Testament has not been abrogated or rendered obsolete but remains necessary for instruction alongside the New Testament. As it is written, *"All scripture is given by inspiration of God, and is profitable for doctrine, for reproof, for correction, for instruction in righteousness,"* (2 Timothy 3:16). When Christ commanded, *"Search the scriptures,"* (John 5:39), He

---

[6] Against Heresies, Book 3, Chapter 11.

referred to the Old Testament, as the New Testament had not yet been written.

Our Savior frequently cited the Old Testament to confirm His teachings, demonstrating its continued authority.

Objection: But some may argue, "The law and the prophets were until John: since that time the kingdom of God is preached," (Luke 16:16).

Solution: The law and the prophets endured until John, not by being abolished but by being fulfilled in the greater light of Christ. The Old Testament contains the same Gospel revealed in the New Testament—the same Spirit, the same Christ, *"Jesus Christ the same yesterday, and today, and forever,"* (Hebrews 13:8). The Old and New Testaments illuminate and affirm each other; the former foretells what the latter confirms has come to pass.

Thirdly, the Scriptures of the Old and New Testaments are perfect and fully sufficient on their own to instruct us in the way of salvation. We are expressly forbidden to add to or subtract from them, as it is written, *"What thing soever I command you, observe to do it: thou shalt not add thereto, nor diminish from it,"* (Deuteronomy 12:32) and *"If any man shall add unto these things, God shall add unto him the plagues that are written in this book: and if any man shall take away from the words of the book of this prophecy, God shall take away his part out of the book of life,"* (Revelation 22:18-19). If any part of Scripture is perfect, how much more so the whole? As the psalmist declares, *"The law of the Lord is perfect, converting the soul,"* (Psalm 19:7).

John wrote, *"These are written, that ye might believe that Jesus is the Christ, the Son of God; and that believing ye might have life through his name,"* (John 20:31). The Scriptures are sufficient to make us wise unto salvation and to thoroughly equip us for every good work (2 Timothy 3:15-17). This sufficiency excludes the need for tradition, for what can be added to that which is already perfect?

Tradition, whether written or unwritten, must align with Scripture. If it agrees with Scripture, it is included within it and must be received as such. If it contradicts Scripture, it must be rejected as the product of a lying spirit. The Spirit of truth cannot contradict the written Word, for He is its Author.

Fourthly, the Scriptures are clear and accessible in all essential matters of faith, so that even the simple and unlearned can and should read them. As it is written, *"For the commandment is a lamp; and the law is light,"* (Proverbs 6:23) and *"The testimony of the Lord is sure, making wise the simple,"* (Psalm 19:7). The psalmist further declares, *"Thy word is a lamp unto my feet, and a light unto my path,"* (Psalm 119:105).

If the Scriptures are a light, they must illuminate and cannot remain hidden except, to those who are lost. Their obscurity lies not in the Scriptures themselves but in the blindness imposed by the god of this world (2 Corinthians 4:3-4). As Paul wrote, *"Whatsoever things were written aforetime were written for our learning,"* (Romans 15:4). To fulfill this purpose, the Scriptures must be clear and comprehensible. If they were inherently dark or ambiguous, how could they serve as a light?

The Scriptures bring forth faith, as it is written, *"These are written, that ye might believe,"* (John 20:31) and *"Faith cometh by hearing, and hearing by the word of God,"* (Romans 10:17). Since faith begins with knowledge, the Scriptures must be plain enough to impart understanding.

Objection: Peter wrote that there are *"some things hard to be understood"* in Paul's letters, which the unlearned wrest to their destruction (2 Peter 3:16).

Solution: The difficulties in certain passages do not endanger *salvation*, as they are explained elsewhere in Scripture. By "unlearned," Peter refers not to those lacking worldly education but to those *ignorant of the Scriptures themselves*. Many simple and uneducated believers have attained saving knowledge through humility, the fear of God, prayer, and diligent study of the Scriptures. The Scriptures interpret themselves, as Augustine noted: *"All things are seen by the light, but light is seen by itself."*

Lastly, the books commonly referred to as the *Apocrypha* are not of divine authority. They were not written by prophets or men inspired by the Holy Spirit and are therefore not part of the Scriptures referred to as *"the scriptures of the prophets"* (Romans 16:26). Christ divided the Scriptures into Moses and the Prophets (Luke 16:29), yet none of the apocryphal books were written by Moses or any of the prophets.

These books often contain vain and contradictory stories, such as those found in *Tobit, the Maccabees*, and *Bel and the Dragon*. The Jews did not include these books in their canon, nor were they accepted as canonical by the early Church or the ancient fathers. Even learned Roman Catholic scholars, such as Arias Montanus, acknowledged their apocryphal status, stating in the preface to his Bible, *"There be added in this edition the books written in Greek, which the Catholic Church, following the canon of the Hebrews, reckoneth amongst the Apocrypha."*

Chapter 2:
Of the Blessed Trinity

There is but one living and true God, eternal and unchanging. Within the unity of this Godhead, there exist three persons—Father, Son, and Holy Spirit—each of one substance, power, and eternity.

This doctrine forms the very foundation of the Christian faith. If this truth is undermined, the entirety of Christian doctrine would inevitably collapse. It is for this reason that the devil has persistently raised up fierce adversaries who oppose the doctrine of the Trinity with strange and blasphemous claims. In the early Church, figures such as Simon Magus, Cerinthus, Ebion, and Manes—a Persian known for his wild fury—stood as enemies of this truth.

Today, the doctrine of the Trinity is opposed by all who deny the divinity of Christ, including unbelieving Jews, Mohammedans, Turks, Moors, and other miscreants. Among those who call themselves Christians, opposition arises from those who have absorbed the doctrines of infidels.

These adversaries can be grouped into two main categories:

1. **Those who deny any distinction of persons within the Godhead.** They claim that the Father, Son, and Holy Spirit are merely different names for one person, used to describe different

actions or roles. This heresy is commonly attributed to Sabellius, though it originated with Noetus, a disciple of Montanus. Even earlier, Simon Magus had laid the groundwork for this false doctrine. In more recent times, M. Erbery, a former chaplain in the army, has revived this teaching. He claimed that there is but one person in the Godhead and that the Father, Son, and Holy Spirit are merely various appearances of God to humanity. His doctrine closely mirrors the teachings of Simon Magus, as noted by St. Augustine (*De Haeresibus*, Chapter 1).

2. **Those who admit the distinction of three persons but deny their equality.** They argue that the Son and the Holy Spirit are not equal to the Father and do not share the same divine essence and eternity. This was the heresy of Arius, who denied the eternal generation of the Son, and of Macedonius, who denied the divinity of the Holy Spirit. These errors have been revived in our own time. M. Biddle, for example, claims to believe in the divinity of the Son but denies the divinity of the Holy Spirit, describing Him merely as an exalted creature, the foremost among ministering spirits.

Mr. Best has also resurrected the heresy of Arius, undeterred by the fearful judgment that befell Arius, who died a sudden and shameful death, his body bursting open like that of Judas Iscariot (Acts 1:18).

Chapter 2: Of the Blessed Trinity

Despite these warnings, Mr. Best has gathered many followers in these times of widespread apostasy.

The origin of these heresies can be traced back to Simon Magus, the impious sorcerer, and their dissemination owes much to Mohammed, an impudent deceiver. Around the year 630 (or, as some claim, 670), Mohammed composed his corrupt book, the *Quran*, filled with impious fables and lies, including blasphemies against the Trinity. From this polluted source, Michael Servetus, a Spaniard, drew his heretical beliefs. Servetus, who was more familiar with Mohammed's law than the Gospel of Christ, denied the eternal Sonship of Christ and was burned at the stake in Geneva around 1530. Yet even from his ashes arose another heretic: Socinus.

Historically, the first nation to defect from the doctrine of the Trinity was Transylvania, a region bordering the Turkish Empire. In an effort to appease their barbarous neighbors, they renounced their belief in the Trinity around 1593, denying the divinity of the Son and the Holy Spirit. This heretical contagion has since spread throughout many parts of Christendom.

The devil has employed countless strategies to undermine this sacred truth, all aimed at stripping Christ of His divinity and thereby destroying the entire foundation of Christianity.

The Antidote to Heresy

To counter these heresies, the doctrine of the Trinity must be upheld in its *fullness*. This defense can be divided into three key propositions:

1. There are three persons in the eternal Godhead: the Father, the Son, and the Holy Spirit.
2. The Son is eternal God, equal to the Father.
3. The Holy Spirit is eternal God, equal to both the Father and the Son.

Each of these truths stands as an essential pillar of Christian doctrine, preserving the Church from the destructive influence of heresy.

The Doctrine of the Trinity and the Divine Nature of the Son

1. The Three Persons in the Godhead. Scripture affirms the plurality of persons within the Godhead. In Genesis 1:26, it is written, *"And God said, Let us make man in our image, after our likeness."* Here, the word *"us"* signifies the plurality of persons, while *"image"* speaks to the unity of essence. Again, in Genesis 3:22: *"And the Lord God said, Behold, the man is become as one of us."* Isaiah 6:8 records: *"Also I heard the voice of the Lord, saying, Whom shall I send, and who will go for us?"* The use of *"I"* demonstrates the unity of essence, and *"us"* confirms the distinction of persons.

In Genesis 19:24, we read: *"Then the Lord rained upon Sodom and upon Gomorrah brimstone and fire from the Lord out of heaven."* Here, one person of the Trinity is clearly distinguished from another. In Hosea 1:6-7, God declares, "*I will no more have mercy upon the house of Israel... But I will have mercy upon the house of Judah, and will save them by the Lord their God.*" Zechariah 2:8-9 and 3:2 also show these distinctions: *"For thus saith the Lord of hosts; After the glory hath he sent me unto the nations... And the Lord said unto Satan, The Lord rebuke thee."*

The plurality is further supported in Psalm 2:7, "The Lord hath said unto me, Thou art my Son; this day have I begotten thee." In Genesis 1:2, the Spirit of God is specifically named: "And the Spirit of God moved upon the face of the waters."

In the New Testament, the Trinity is made explicit. At Christ's baptism, "the heavens were opened unto him, and he saw the Spirit of God descending like a dove, and lighting upon him: and lo a voice from heaven, saying, This is my beloved Son, in whom I am well pleased," (Matthew 3:16-17). The baptismal formula in Matthew 28:19 instructs believers to be baptized "in the name of the Father, and of the Son, and of the Holy Ghost." Similarly, 1 John 5:7 declares: "For there are three that bear record in heaven, the Father, the Word, and the Holy Ghost: and these three are one."

This truth, once more obscure, became clearer with time, like the morning light growing until full day. Initially, Scripture intimates the plurality of persons; later, the Trinity is explicitly named. Finally, Scripture provides distinct interactions between these persons. For instance, John 5:32, 37 states: *"There is another that beareth witness of me... And the Father himself, which hath sent me, hath borne witness of me.*" In John 14:16-17, Christ speaks of the Comforter: "*And I will pray the Father, and he shall give you another Comforter, that he may abide with you forever; even the Spirit of truth.*" The word "*another*" emphasizes the distinction between the Father, Son, and Holy Spirit—three distinct persons sharing one undivided essence.

John 15:26 confirms: "But when the Comforter is come, whom I will send unto you from the Father, even the Spirit of truth, which proceedeth from the Father, he shall testify of me." Similarly, John 16:28 says: "I came forth from the Father, and am come into the world." These statements of "coming forth" reveal the personal distinctions within the Godhead, each person having a true and distinct subsistence.

Thus, the doctrine is upheld: three persons in one Godhead—distinct but not divided, separate in person yet unified in essence, according to 1 John 5:7, "*And these three are one.*"

Objection: Some argue that this text refers to an agreement in testimony rather than an essential unity, citing verse 8: "*And there are three that bear witness in earth... and these three agree in one.*"

Solution: The Apostle contrasts the heavenly and earthly witnesses—the testimony of men versus the testimony of God. The earthly witnesses—water, blood, and spirit—are three distinct elements that agree in one message but remain separate. In contrast, the heavenly witnesses—the Father, Word, and Holy Spirit—are three persons who, though distinct in number, are one in nature and essence. Therefore, the testimony in heaven is of one God.

2. The Son as Eternal God. Isaiah 53:8 asks: "Who shall declare his generation?" John 1:14, 18 affirms the Son's divine origin: "And the Word was made flesh, and dwelt among us... No man hath seen God at any time; the only begotten Son, which is in the bosom of the Father, he hath declared him." 1 John 4:9 adds: "In this was manifested the love of God toward us, because that God sent his only begotten Son into the world, that we might live through him."

The Son is not a child of grace, like the angels by creation or believers by adoption. He is the *only begotten* Son. As Hebrews 1:5 asks: *"For unto which of the angels said he at any time, Thou art my Son, this day have I begotten thee?"* Though the angels are sons of God by creation, the Son of God is unique in His eternal generation. Romans 8:32 calls Him *"his own Son."* Since God is indivisible in essence, the Son must possess the fullness of the Father's essence, not merely a portion, making Him one with the Father in *divine nature.*

Scripture explicitly names the Son as *God.* Isaiah 9:6 declares: "For unto us a child is born... and his name shall be called... The mighty God." Titus 2:13 refers to Him as: "The great God and our Saviour Jesus Christ." 1 John 5:20 states: "This is the true God, and eternal life." Romans 9:5 calls Him: "God blessed for ever." Psalm 40:7

and Hebrews 1:8 say: "Thy throne, O God, is for ever and ever."

The works of creation and preservation, which belong to God alone, are ascribed to the Son. John 1:3 states: *"All things were made by him; and without him was not any thing made that was made."* Hebrews 1:3 affirms that *"all things"* are upheld by His power. In Matthew 9:2, Christ forgives sins: *"Son, be of good cheer; thy sins be forgiven thee."* In John 10:28, He gives eternal life: *"And I give unto them eternal life; and they shall never perish."* John 5:19 declares: *"For what things soever he [the Father] doeth, these also doeth the Son likewise."*

The Son also possesses the attributes of God: omnipotence (Revelation 1:8), eternity (Isaiah 9:6), and omniscience (John 21:17). He is described as being equal with the Father: *"But said also that God was his Father, making himself equal with God,"* (John 5:18). Philippians 2:6 affirms: *"Who, being in the form of God, thought it not robbery to be equal with God."*

Thus, Scripture bears consistent and irrefutable witness to the eternal divinity of the Son, confirming His coequality and coeternity with the Father.

Divine Worship Given to the Son

Divine worship, which is due to God alone, is given to the Son. Psalm 97:7 commands: "Worship him, all ye gods." Hebrews 1:6 reiterates: "And again, when he bringeth in the firstbegotten into the world, he saith,

And let all the angels of God worship him." Such worship would be outright idolatry if Christ were merely a creature. In John 5:23, it is stated: "That all men should honour the Son, even as they honour the Father." The same honor and reverence given to the Father is due to the Son.

The Apostles identified themselves as servants of Jesus Christ. Paul writes: *"Paul, a servant of Jesus Christ, called to be an apostle,"* (Romans 1:1). Peter likewise professes: *"Simon Peter, a servant and an apostle of Jesus Christ,"* (2 Peter 1:1). Jude introduces himself in the same way: *"Jude, the servant of Jesus Christ,"* (Jude 1:1). John, too, in Revelation 1:1 describes: *"The revelation of Jesus Christ, which God gave unto him... and he sent and signified it by his angel unto his servant John."*

Believers are commanded to place their trust in Christ. Isaiah 11:10 declares: "And in that day there shall be a root of Jesse, which shall stand for an ensign of the people; to it shall the Gentiles seek." Romans 15:12 reiterates this: "In him shall the Gentiles trust." Christ Himself says in John 14:1: "Ye believe in God, believe also in me." Psalm 2:12 proclaims: "Blessed are all they that put their trust in him." This command to trust in the Son stands in contrast to the warning in Jeremiah 17:5-7, "Cursed be the man that trusteth in man, and maketh flesh his arm, and whose heart departeth from the Lord." Therefore, it is evident that the Son is equal with the Father and deserving of divine worship.

The Holy Spirit as God Everlasting

1. The Divine Titles of the Holy Spirit. The Holy Spirit is referred to explicitly as both *Lord* and *God*. In 1 Corinthians 12:5-6, it is written: *"And there are differences of administrations, but the same Lord... and there are diversities of operations, but it is the same God which worketh all in all."* Isaiah 40:13-18 also attributes divine titles to the Spirit: *"Who hath directed the Spirit of the Lord, or being his counsellor hath taught him?"* Isaiah 6:9 is echoed in Acts 28:25-26, where the Spirit is shown as speaking divine words. Psalm 95 is compared with Hebrews 3 to show that the Holy Spirit is called *"the Lord our Maker."* Leviticus 26:12-13, 1 Corinthians 3:16, 1 Corinthians 6:19, and 2 Corinthians 6:16 all describe our bodies as the *"temples of the living God"* and specifically as temples of the Holy Spirit. If the Holy Spirit were not God, such language would be inappropriate, as a temple is reserved solely for divine worship. Augustine writes: "If we were commanded to build him a temple of wood and stone, it would be a clear proof of his Godhead, for this service is only due unto God; how much more, then, when our very bodies are called his temple."[7]

2. The Divine Attributes of the Holy Spirit Divine attributes are ascribed to the Holy Spirit. He is omniscient, as stated in 1 Corinthians 2:10: *"But God hath revealed them unto us by his Spirit: for the Spirit searcheth all*

---

[7] *Contra Maximinum Arianum*, Book 1.

things, yea, the deep things of God." He is omnipresent, as described in Psalm 139:7: *"Whither shall I go from thy spirit? or whither shall I flee from thy presence?"* He is eternal, as Hebrews 9:14 says: *"How much more shall the blood of Christ, who through the eternal Spirit offered himself without spot to God, purge your conscience from dead works to serve the living God?"* Foreknowledge, which God claims as a unique mark of His divinity, is also attributed to the Holy Spirit. Isaiah 41:23 challenges false gods to prove their divinity by foretelling future events. Yet this power belongs solely to the Holy Spirit, as demonstrated in 2 Samuel 23:2: *"The Spirit of the Lord spake by me, and his word was in my tongue,"* and in Acts 1:16: *"This scripture must needs have been fulfilled, which the Holy Ghost by the mouth of David spake before concerning Judas."* Paul further warns in 1 Timothy 4:1: *"Now the Spirit speaketh expressly, that in the latter times some shall depart from the faith."*

3. The Divine Works of the Holy Spirit

The Holy Spirit performs works that belong exclusively to God. These include:

- **Creation:** "By his spirit he hath garnished the heavens," (Job 26:13); "The Spirit of God hath made me, and the breath of the Almighty hath given me life," (Job 33:4).
- **Preservation:** "And the Spirit of God moved upon the face of the waters," (Genesis 1:2).
- **Regeneration and Sanctification:** "Except a man be born of water and of the Spirit, he cannot

enter into the kingdom of God," (John 3:5); "According to his mercy he saved us, by the washing of regeneration, and renewing of the Holy Ghost," (Titus 3:5); "But ye are washed, but ye are sanctified... by the Spirit of our God," (1 Corinthians 6:11).
- **Raising the Dead:** "But if the Spirit of him that raised up Jesus from the dead dwell in you, he that raised up Christ from the dead shall also quicken your mortal bodies by his Spirit that dwelleth in you," (Romans 8:11).

The second general council under Emperor Theodosius the Great condemned Macedonius, who denied the divinity of the Holy Spirit, stating: *"If he were created, how does he create? How does he sanctify? How does he give life? These are not the works of a creature but the works of the great and mighty God."*

Lastly, the very name *Spirit* reveals His nature. Just as the spirit of man is of the nature of man, the Spirit of God is of the nature of God—not a part of God, as the human spirit is part of man, but the fullness of the divine essence. The Holy Spirit is called the Spirit of the Son as well as the Spirit of the Father and is said to be sent by both. This demonstrates the essential unity of the Trinity, showing that the Father, Son, and Holy Spirit are one God.

The Christian faith declares: "We worship one God in Trinity, and Trinity in Unity; neither confounding the persons nor dividing the substance.

Chapter 2: Of the Blessed Trinity

The Father is God, the Son is God, and the Holy Ghost is God; yet they are not three Gods, but one God. For the Godhead of the Father, of the Son, and of the Holy Ghost is all one, the glory equal, the majesty coeternal. In this Trinity, none is before or after the other, none is greater or lesser than the other." The Athanasian Creed rightly affirms: "He that will be saved must thus think of the Trinity."[8]

---

[8] Athanas. *Symb.*

Chapter 3:
Of the Creation

"In the beginning, God created the heaven and the earth," (Genesis 1:1).

God made all things—both visible and invisible—by His infinite power. Man, however, was formed uniquely from the dust of the ground. He was not created corrupt or sinful, as he later became, but was made in the likeness and image of God, reflecting true holiness and perfect happiness.

In earlier times, various erroneous beliefs about the creation arose. These errors, though less common now, were once propagated by figures such as Simon Magus, Cerinthus, Marcion, and Manicheus, among others. Today, the resurgence of some of these errors can be seen.

1. The Anthropomorphites (those who ascribe bodily form to God). This group interprets the phrase "made in the likeness of God," to mean that God possesses a body shaped like a human form. Epiphanius attributes this belief to ignorance and calls them schismatics rather than heretics. Similarly, the Messalian heretics claimed that God could be seen with physical eyes, misinterpreting Christ's words in Matthew 5:8: "Blessed are the pure in heart: for they shall see God." In the present day, some assert that Adam was created in the personal shape of God and that God

has a visible, personal form that He can make manifest at will.

2. The Doctrine of Osiander. Osiander taught that man was made like God by receiving an infusion of the divine substance—a notion borrowed from the Manichees and Priscillianists. The Manichees taught that man's body was made from the substance of the prince of darkness, while the soul was part of the divine essence. E. Avery, in a publication from 1647, advanced a similar error, asserting that the rational soul in all humans is God Himself. The Familists echo this belief, claiming that "Adam was all that God was, and God was all that Adam was."

The Roman Catholics also hold erroneous beliefs concerning the image of God in Adam, original righteousness, the location of paradise, and the nature of the tree of life.

Man's Nature in Creation

Man was created after the completion of heaven and earth, formed as a creature reflecting both heavenly and earthly qualities. His soul was heavenly, immortal, and capable of communion with God, while his body was earthly, made from the dust. In this way, man became a representation of the whole creation—a microcosm.

When Scripture says that man was made in the "image of God," it does not imply that his physical form resembles God. God is a Spirit (John 4:24), without body, form, or visible features, and is therefore referred to as "the invisible God," (Colossians 1:15).

However, man bears the image of God in the following ways:

1. The grace and majesty of the human form: Man's body excels that of other creatures, reflecting a dignity that hints at divine majesty.

2. The nature of the soul: the soul is immortal, like God. The soul possesses understanding and will, endowed with divine graces such as wisdom, knowledge, righteousness, and true holiness. This spiritual likeness is emphasized in Ephesians 4:23-24: "And be renewed in the spirit of your mind; and that ye put on the new man, which after God is created in righteousness and true holiness." Similarly, Colossians 3:10 says: "And have put on the new man, which is renewed in knowledge after the image of him that created him."

3. Dominion over creation: at creation, man was given authority over the other creatures, as stated in Genesis 1:28: "Be fruitful, and multiply, and replenish the earth, and subdue it: and have dominion over the fish of the sea, and over the fowl of the air, and over every living thing that moveth upon the earth." In this way, man was like a lesser god to the creatures, just as magistrates are referred to as "gods" in Psalm 82:6: "I have said, Ye are gods; and all of you are children of the most High."

Refutation of Heresies

The very term "image" proves that man's soul is not God Himself nor any part of the divine essence, for nothing can be an image of itself. The soul of man is an immortal nature, created out of nothing by the power of God and breathed into the body. Furthermore, Scripture warns that the souls of the wicked shall perish eternally in hell, as declared in Matthew 10:28: "Fear him which is able to destroy both soul and body in hell." This proves that the soul, though immortal, is not divine in substance but a creation of God.

In this way, the doctrine of creation affirms that man was made in the image of God, not by sharing in the divine essence but by reflecting His righteousness, holiness, and dominion in a creaturely form.

Chapter 4: Of Divine Providence

God, having created the world out of nothing, did not abandon it to its own course but continues to sustain and govern all things by His almighty power and wisdom. He preserves all that exists and orders all that occurs according to His own good pleasure, so that nothing happens by chance or without purpose, but all things unfold according to the counsel of His divine will.

Adversaries to the Doctrine of Providence

1. Atheists and Epicureans deny the existence of divine providence, claiming that all things come about by chance or fortune.

2. Stoics and supporters of fatalism assert a rigid chain of second causes, effectively binding God's hands and denying Him the liberty to change or direct events according to His will.

3. Familists argue that nature governs all things.

4. Free-will proponents hold that certain matters fall under human control, independent of divine providence.

5. Worldly-minded individuals attribute their success to their own wisdom and efforts.

6. Those who belittle God's care claim that His providence does not extend to trivial matters, deeming such concerns unworthy of His majesty, much as a prince might disregard the affairs of his kitchen.

Chapter 4: Of Divine Providence

The Doctrine of Providence

The belief in divine providence is confirmed by the existence of an infinitely wise and powerful God. Were anything to occur by chance, or apart from His will, His omniscience and omnipotence would be undermined. Scripture bears abundant witness to this truth: "The eyes of the Lord are in every place," (Proverbs 15:3). Who humbleth himself to behold the things that are in heaven, and in the earth," (Psalm 113:6). "Whatsoever the Lord pleased, that did he in heaven, and in earth," (Psalm 135:6). "Yea, before the day was, I am he; and there is none that can deliver out of my hand: I will work, and who shall let it?" (Isaiah 43:13).

Aspects of Divine Providence

1. God orders all things freely according to His will. God is under no compulsion but acts according to His own good pleasure. He may even act contrary to the established course of nature, as seen when He caused the sun to stand still at Joshua's command (Joshua 10:13) and to move backward at Hezekiah's request (2 Kings 20:11). These miracles show that the laws of nature are merely ordinances established by Him, which He can suspend or alter at will. All second causes are like links in a chain, upheld and directed by divine providence.

2. Providence extends to all creatures. God's care encompasses even the lowliest of beings: "These wait all upon thee, that thou mayest give them their meat in due season," (Psalm 104:27). "He giveth to the beast his food,

and to the young ravens which cry," (Psalm 147:9). God's providence is over both peasants and princes: "God standeth in the congregation of the mighty," (Psalm 82:1). He raises the lowly and delivers the oppressed: "He raiseth up the poor out of the dust," (Psalm 113:7). "The Lord looketh from heaven; he beholdeth all the sons of men," (Psalm 33:13).

3. Providence governs even casual events. Seemingly random occurrences fall under God's direction. "The lot is cast into the lap; but the whole disposing thereof is of the Lord," (Proverbs 16:33).

4. Providence extends to trivial matters. Even the smallest details are subject to His care: "Are not two sparrows sold for a farthing? and one of them shall not fall on the ground without your Father... But the very hairs of your head are all numbered," (Matthew 10:29-30).

5. Providence encompasses sinful actions. Even the wicked actions of men are within God's sovereign control. Acts 4:28 declares that all done against Christ occurred according to "whatsoever thy hand and thy counsel determined before to be done." Though God permits sin, He remains just and pure, turning the evil intent of sinners to serve His purposes for His glory and the good of His people.

Objection: If God has a role in sinful actions, does this make Him the author of sin?

Solution: By no means. God does not infuse evil or malice into anyone. "In him we live, and move, and have our being," (Acts 17:28), but the disposition to sin comes from the corrupt nature of man, not from God. Just as the earth nourishes all trees, but the fault for producing bitter fruit lies with the tree itself, so too God's sustaining power does not make Him responsible for sinful deeds. He remains holy and just, as Paul argues: "Is God unrighteous who taketh vengeance? God forbid: for then how shall God judge the world?" (Romans 3:5-6).

The Scope of Divine Providence

All things in creation—whether angels or men, animals or devils—are subject to God's providence. He governs all people, high and low, in every aspect of their lives: their actions, both natural and voluntary, good and evil, as well as their persons, lives, liberties, and possessions. Nothing is hidden from His sight, nothing occurs by chance, and nothing is so trivial that it escapes His notice.

God's works are great and marvelous, encompassing even those things done against His will. Augustine explains: "That which is done against His will could not occur unless He permitted it. Yet He permits it not unwillingly, but willingly, for He is good and Almighty and would not allow evil to be done unless He could bring good out of it."[9]

---

[9] Enchiridion, Chapter 100.

Thus, divine providence rules over all things, ensuring that nothing happens apart from God's wise and sovereign will.

Chapter 5:
Of the Fall of Man, and of Original sin

Our first parents, Adam and Eve, were created in a perfect and blessed state—both holy and happy. However, through their own voluntary disobedience in eating the forbidden fruit, contrary to God's command, they fell from that state and plunged themselves and all their descendants into an opposite condition of sin and death. Since that tragic fall, the image of God has been defaced in all humanity. Every person is conceived in sin and born a child of wrath (Psalm 51:5; Eph. 2:3).

Errors Concerning Original Sin

Some have sought to downplay Adam's sin and its consequences:

1. Minimization of Adam's Sin: Some claim that Adam's sin was merely a matter of satisfying an unrestrained appetite.

2. Pelagian Denial of Original Sin: Pelagius and his followers *denied* the doctrine of original sin, asserting that Adam's sin harmed only himself and did not affect his descendants. They taught that no one is condemned in hell because of Adam's sin and that sin is passed down only by imitation, not by natural descent. They further claimed that infants inherit no sin from their parents

and therefore do not need baptism. The Anabaptists follow in their footsteps.

    3. Roman Catholic View: The Roman Catholics acknowledge original sin but severely diminish its seriousness. They assert that concupiscence (the inclination to sin that remains after baptism) is not truly sin but merely an inclination or the material cause from which sin arises. The Council of Trent decreed that anyone who says otherwise is to be anathematized.[10]

These erroneous views are subtle deceptions of the devil, aimed at hiding the true nature of the disease to make it incurable.

The Gravity of Adam's Sin

Adam's sin was not a minor offense but an act of grievous rebellion against God. By examining its nature, we see how many sins were contained within this one act:

    1. Intolerable pride and ambition: Adam was not content with the divine image stamped upon him—he sought to be equal with God in majesty. As the serpent said, "Ye shall be as gods," (Genesis 3:5).

    2. Ingratitude: Despite the abundance of all other creatures freely given for their use, Adam was ungrateful.

    3. Apostasy: In his rebellion, Adam turned away from God to align with the devil, God's enemy.

---

[10] Council of Trent, Session 5, Chapter 1.

4. Unbelief: Adam's unbelief undergirded all the other sins. He disregarded God's promise and command and instead believed the devil's claim that God was deceitful, envious, and untrustworthy (Genesis 3:4-5).

Therefore, this sin cannot be measured merely by the physical act of eating the forbidden fruit or reduced to an excess of natural appetite. Adam's fall was a profound act of defiance that brought death and corruption to all his descendants.

The Nature and Transmission of Original Sin

1. Definition of Original Sin: Original sin is so called because it begins with our very existence—present from the moment of our conception and birth. As David confesses: "Behold, I was shapen in iniquity; and in sin did my mother conceive me," (Psalm 51:5). This sin is passed down to all humanity in two ways: through the guilt of Adam's transgression and through the corruption of our nature.

2. The Guilt of Adam's Transgression: The guilt of Adam's sin is imputed to his descendants. As Paul writes: "By one man's disobedience many were made sinners," (Romans 5:19). "By the offense of one, judgment came upon all men to condemnation," (Romans 5:18). "By one man's offense, death reigned by one," (Romans 5:17). Just as Levi, being in Abraham's loins, paid tithes to Melchizedek (Hebrews 7:9), so all humanity, being in Adam, shared in his sin.

3. The Corruption of Nature: The corruption of human nature is passed down by natural generation. Adam, as the root and representative of all humanity, could only pass on what he had become after the fall. "Who can bring a clean thing out of an unclean? not one," (Job 14:4). This original corruption manifests as:

1. Inability and aversion to good: Humanity, by nature, is incapable of seeking or doing true good (Romans 7:14).

2. Inclination to evil: We are predisposed to all manner of sin (Romans 7:23).

4. The Extent of Corruption: Every part of the human being is affected: Understanding: Darkened (1 Corinthians 2:14). Conscience: Numb and insensitive (Ephesians 4:19). Will: In bondage to sin (Romans 7:23). Affections: Disordered and self-serving (James 4:1-2). Body: The members are instruments of sin (Romans 3:13-15; Romans 6:19). In this way, when Adam begat a son, it is recorded: "And Adam... begat a son in his own likeness, after his image," (Genesis 5:3)—no longer bearing the pure image of God but a corrupted likeness.

5. Evidence of Original Sin in Infants: Although infants have not committed personal, willful sins, they still suffer the consequences of original sin, as seen in their mortality. Paul affirms: "Death passed upon all men, for that all have sinned," (Romans 5:12). "The wages of sin is death," (Romans 6:23). If infants were free from sin, they would not be subject to death.

6. The Necessity of Regeneration: Jesus declared: "Except a man be born again, he cannot see the kingdom of God," (John 3:3). He explained: "That which is born of the flesh is flesh," (John 3:6). This necessity for a new birth proves the corruption of our natural state. If humans were born free from sin, there would be no need for this second birth.

Even those who are regenerated still contend with the remnants of original sin, as Paul laments: "I am carnal, sold under sin," (Romans 7:14). The ongoing struggle between the flesh and the Spirit is evident: "For the flesh lusteth against the Spirit, and the Spirit against the flesh," (Galatians 5:17).

Chapter 6: Of Freewill

Since the tragic fall of our first parents, Adam and Eve, the nature of humanity has been *entirely* corrupted. Because of this, the entire human race has been brought into miserable bondage under sin. No person, by any natural power within themselves, is able to believe in God or turn toward Him, nor can they will, think, or perform anything truly good or acceptable in the sight of God.

Errors Concerning Freewill

1. Philosophical Influence: The belief in freewill, as it relates to spiritual matters, originated from certain ancient philosophers and later infiltrated Christian doctrine.

2. Pelagianism: Taught first by Pelagius and followed by Anabaptists, Arminians, Socinians, and Roman Catholics, this doctrine asserts that natural humanity possesses the ability and freedom to choose and obey God's commandments and reject sin by their own strength.

Their reasoning is as follows: God's law would be given in vain if people had no capacity to obey it. Exhortations, precepts, promises, and threats would be meaningless if obedience were impossible. It would be unjust for God to punish individuals for failing to perform duties that are beyond their power. Pelagians claim that the fall merely weakened human will rather than rendering it completely unable, asserting that grace is merely an aid to strengthen the weak nature.

The Biblical Teaching on Freewill

While humanity remains a rational being capable of receiving grace and retains the faculties of understanding and will, Scripture teaches that, after the fall, these faculties were corrupted and darkened.

The Four States of Humanity: 1. Creation: In the state of creation, humanity was holy and upright. 2. Corruption: After the fall, humanity was rendered incapable of turning to God or doing good. 3. Renovation: In the state of regeneration, the redeemed are renewed and empowered by God's grace. 4. Glorification: In the final state of glory, believers are made perfect and freed from all sin.

The question at hand concerns the second state—humanity's natural condition after the fall. According to Scripture, fallen humanity has no power to convert themselves or do good. Consider the following passages: "Not that we are sufficient of ourselves to think anything as of ourselves; but our sufficiency is of God," (2 Corinthians 3:5). "For it is God which worketh in you both to will and to do of his good pleasure," (Philippians 2:13). "And you hath he quickened, who were dead in trespasses and sins," (Ephesians 2:1). "Without me ye can do nothing," (John 15:5). "No man can come to me, except the Father which hath sent me draw him," (John 6:44).

Testimonies from the Church Fathers:

The Council of Orange stated: "If man could not retain what he had received without the grace of God, how can he recover it without the same grace after losing it?"

Ambrose wrote: "Let no man trust in his own strength, which failed him even when it was whole."

Bernard declared: "It would have been better not to have existed than to be left to the control of our own will. It is not the devil's power that enslaves us, but our own will; it is God's grace that makes us free."

Objections and Responses:

Objection 1: If humanity lacks the power to do good, is it not unjust for God to demand obedience?

Response: Not at all. When God created humanity, He endowed them with the ability to obey. Humanity lost that ability through voluntary sin, as stated in Ecclesiastes 7:29: "God hath made man upright; but they have sought out many inventions." It is not unjust for God to require what was originally given to humanity, even though it has been squandered.

Objection 2: If humanity has no power to do good, what purpose do exhortations, admonitions, precepts, promises, and preaching serve?

Response: These are not in vain but are the means ordained by God to soften hearts and incline the will toward Him. Paul writes: "For it is God which worketh in you both to will and to do of his good pleasure," (Philippians 2:13), yet Paul continues to exhort believers to obedience. Likewise, Jesus repeatedly invites people to come to Him, while also declaring: "No man can come to me, except the Father which hath sent me draw him," (John 6:44).

In this way, divine grace is both the source and sustainer of the believer's will and actions, making the call to obedience meaningful and effectual.

Chapter 7: Of Christ's Person

In this miserable and helpless condition of being under the fall of Adam, God in His mercy did not abandon humanity to despair but sent His Son to take on human nature. Being both fully God and fully man, He came to fully satisfy for our sins and redeem our souls from death and hell.

Enemies of Christ

The adversaries of Christ are divided into two groups: 1. Enemies of His Person. 2. Enemies of His Office.

Enemies of His Person

Among those who opposed Christ's person were early heretics such as Simon Magus, Cerinthus, Marcion, Samosatenus, Arius, and Nestorius—monstrous figures who distorted His true nature: Some denied His divinity. Others denied His humanity. Some denied the purity of His conception. Others denied the truth of His incarnation altogether. Some confused the two natures, denying their distinction. Others divided His person, making Him into two separate persons. Some claimed that He took a body but not a soul. Others asserted that He assumed an ethereal or spiritual body rather than a true physical one.

Today, these errors are perpetuated by unbelieving Jews, Turks, all Mohammedans,

Antitrinitarians, New-Arians, Anabaptists, Familists, and Socinians. Among these, figures like Paul Best and others explicitly deny the divinity of Christ, calling Him a mere man. Some go further, accusing Him of being sinful. Others claim He became God only after His incarnation, gaining divinity by merit, office, or extraordinary gifts rather than by nature and eternal generation.

Anabaptist Doctrine: The Anabaptists argue that Christ brought His flesh from heaven and did not take it from the Virgin Mary.

Familist Allegory: The Familists reduce the incarnation to an allegory, claiming that each member of their sect is "Christ" and that their personal acceptance of belief constitutes the incarnation. One of their members, in conversation, claimed: "Christ is now come in my flesh, and when I speak, Christ speaks to you."

Erbery's Doctrine: Erbery taught that "flesh" refers not to Christ's human nature but to the manifestation of the Godhead in the flesh of the saints.

The True Doctrine of Christ's Person

1. Christ Is True God: "Unto us a child is born... and his name shall be called... The mighty God," (Isaiah 9:6). "Of whom as concerning the flesh Christ came, who is over all, God blessed forever," (Romans 9:5). "God was manifest in the flesh," (1 Timothy 3:16). "Declared to be the Son of God with power," (Romans 1:4).

2. Christ Is True Man: He took on a true body from the Virgin Mary and is often referred to as the Son of Man. "For there is one God, and one mediator between God and men, the man Christ Jesus," (1 Timothy 2:5). "A virgin shall conceive and bear a Son," (Isaiah 7:14). "She was found with child by the Holy Ghost," (Matthew 1:20). "Made of a woman," (Galatians 4:4). "That which we have seen with our eyes, which we have looked upon, and our hands have handled, of the Word of life," (1 John 1:1). Christ's humanity was tangible and perceptible to all the senses.

The Necessity of Worshiping Christ as God

If Christ is not truly God, why do we *adore* Him? Worshiping Christ, if He is not God, would be idolatry. Cyril of Alexandria refuted Eunomius by stating that if Christ were merely a man, worshiping Him would constitute idolatry. The second Council of Nicaea condemned Nestorius for idolatry because he claimed Christ was a mere man and yet worshiped Him. Paul condemned the worship of creatures (Romans 1:25) yet professed himself a servant of Jesus Christ (Romans 1:1), indicating that Christ is no mere creature.

The Inconsistency of Modern Denials

The Arians, Socinians, and others who deny Christ's deity yet affirm His worthiness to be worshiped are no different from pagans who worship created beings. Paul denounced such practices: "Professing themselves to be wise, they became fools, and changed the glory of the uncorruptible God into an image made like to corruptible man," (Romans 1:22-25).

Those who, like the heathen, refuse to glorify Christ as God yet give Him divine honor are similarly vain in their imaginations, and their foolish hearts are darkened.

Chapter 8: Of Christ's Office

In this fallen and helpless condition, God did not leave humanity without hope but sent His Son, Jesus Christ, to act as the Mediator between God and mankind, reconciling them to each other. This reconciliation was necessary because God is justly angered by sin, and humanity stands guilty before Him.

Christ's office as Mediator is threefold:
1. Prophet: He instructs His Church in the truth.
2. Priest: He offers satisfaction for sin and continually intercedes for His people.
3. King: He gathers, protects, and governs His Church.

Errors Concerning Christ's Office
Various groups have denied or distorted Christ's role as Mediator:
1. Osiander's Error: Osiander taught that Christ is Mediator only in respect to His divine nature.[11]
2. Stancarus' Error: Stancarus claimed that Christ mediates only in His human nature.
3. The Roman Catholic Error: The Roman Catholic Church errs by assigning mediatorial roles to saints and angels, praying to them for intercession.

---

[11] August. lib. 2. Cont. Epist. Parmen. cap. 8

The Roman Catholic Church also opposes each aspect of Christ's office: His Kingly Office: By making the Pope the head of the Church, they usurp Christ's rightful role as King. His Priestly Office: By establishing other mediators and offering additional forms of satisfaction for sin apart from Christ, they undermine His unique and perfect sacrifice. His Prophetic Office: By subjecting the Holy Scriptures to the authority of the Church and the Pope, they elevate human traditions and inventions to the same level as divine revelation.

The True Doctrine of Christ's Mediatorship

1. Christ Is the Only Mediator: "For there is one God, and one mediator between God and men, the man Christ Jesus," (1 Timothy 2:5). "Who is he that condemneth? It is Christ that died, yea rather, that is risen again, who is even at the right hand of God, who also maketh intercession for us," (Romans 8:34). "He ever liveth to make intercession for them," (Hebrews 7:25).

The saints cannot hear our prayers or know our needs: "Doubtless thou art our father, though Abraham be ignorant of us, and Israel acknowledge us not," (Isaiah 63:16). "The dead know not anything," (Ecclesiastes 9:5). "Call now, if there be any that will answer thee; and to which of the saints wilt thou turn?" (Job 5:1).

If Paul were a mediator, then all the apostles would also be mediators. But Paul himself declared that there is only *one* Mediator (1 Timothy 2:5). Augustine, in his writings against Parmenianus, affirms this singular role of Christ.[12]

2. Christ Mediates According to Both Natures: In His human nature, Christ suffered and died for our sins. In His divine nature, He conquered death and rose again. Without His humanity, He could not have suffered; without His divinity, His suffering would not have had infinite value. Thus, it is written: "Feed the church of God, which he hath purchased with his own blood," (Acts 20:28). Both natures work together in perfect harmony to fulfill His mediatorial role, each performing its proper function while producing one unified effect.

---

[12] August. lib. 2. *Cont. Epist. Parmen.* cap. 8.

Chapter 9: The Death of Christ

The office of Christ as Mediator consists of three parts, with His priestly role being the most central. The heart of His priestly office is His self-oblation upon the Cross, where, as the one and only sacrifice for sin, He appeased the wrath of God and redeemed our souls from eternal death, securing for us the favor of God and everlasting life.

The following groups have opposed or distorted the doctrine of Christ's death:

1. Arians and Socinians: These groups claim that Christ's death did not satisfy divine justice for our sins.

2. Roman Catholics: While acknowledging that Christ's death atones for sin and eternal punishment, they assert that believers must atone for temporal punishment themselves, either in this life or in purgatory.

3. Arminians: They teach that Christ died for all men, both those who are saved and those who perish, including Cain and Judas as well as Abel and Peter. From this view arises the belief that those for whom Christ died may still be lost.

The True Doctrine of the Death of Christ

1. Christ's Death as Satisfaction for Sin: "He was wounded for our transgressions, he was bruised for our iniquities: the chastisement of our peace was upon him; and with his stripes we are healed," (Isaiah 53:5). "For

the transgression of my people was he stricken," (Isaiah 53:8). "Thou shalt make his soul an offering for sin," (Isaiah 53:10). "Even as the Son of man came... to give his life a ransom for many," (Matthew 20:28). "Christ our Passover is sacrificed for us," (1 Corinthians 5:7). "Who was delivered for our offences," (Romans 4:25). "We were reconciled to God by the death of his Son," (Romans 5:10). "Who his own self bare our sins in his own body on the tree," (1 Peter 2:24).

Objection: "Who is a God like unto thee, that pardoneth iniquity, because he delighteth in mercy?" (Micah 7:18). If Christ satisfied for sin, how is it mercy?

Solution: Christ's merits and God's mercy align perfectly. Though Christ satisfied divine justice, our forgiveness remains free to us because God exacts nothing from us, only from Christ. We contribute nothing to our redemption—it is entirely a gift of grace.

2. Christ Satisfied Both Eternal and Temporal Punishment: If believers had to satisfy for some portion of their sin, it would imply that Christ's sacrifice was insufficient. Yet Scripture affirms that He alone bore the full weight of divine wrath: "I have trodden the winepress alone; and of the people there was none with me," (Isaiah 63:3). It would be contrary to God's mercy to demand further satisfaction after fully pardoning sin. It would contradict His justice to forgive the guilt of sin but still require additional punishment.

3. Christ Died Exclusively for the Elect: "He shall save his people from their sins," (Matthew 1:21). "I lay down my life for the sheep," (John 10:15). "I pray for them: I pray not for the world, but for them which thou hast given me," (John 17:9).

4. The Security of the Redeemed: "And I give unto them eternal life; and they shall never perish," (John 10:28). "Who are kept by the power of God through faith unto salvation," (1 Peter 1:5). The power of God cannot be thwarted.

Objection: "Who gave himself a ransom for all," (1 Timothy 2:6); "that he by the grace of God should taste death for every man," (Hebrews 2:9); "And he is the propitiation for our sins: and not for ours only, but also for the sins of the whole world," (1 John 2:2).

Solution: In these verses, "world" refers to the world of God's elect, as seen in John 6:33 and John 17:9. "All" refers to all sorts and degrees of men from every nation, not the entirety of humanity. Augustine explains that "He spared not his own Son, but delivered him up for us all," (Romans 8:32) means "for the elect," as confirmed in the following verse: "Who shall lay anything to the charge of God's elect?" (Romans 8:33). *Augustine* further expounds in his writings against the Donatists that Christ's propitiation applies to the "wheat" that grows throughout the world, not the "tares."

In this way, Christ's death was not a universal provision for all individuals but a particular redemption for His people, securing their salvation fully and eternally.

Chapter 10: The Resurrection of Christ

Christ truly rose again from the dead, taking up His body—flesh, bones, and all that pertains to the perfection of human nature. With this same body, He ascended into Heaven and now sits at the right hand of God until He returns to judge the world at the end of time.

Several false doctrines have arisen to deny or distort the truth of Christ's resurrection:

1. David George and his followers: They claimed that Christ's body was dissolved into ashes and did not rise again—an ancient error echoed by Apelles, who taught that Christ's body returned to the four elements from which it was composed.

2. The Swenkfeldians: They asserted that Christ's human body was completely laid aside.

3. The Ubiquitarians: They claimed that Christ's body is everywhere, just as His divine nature is.

4. Sun Worshippers: Some have revived the Manichean and Seleucian heresy, teaching that Christ left His body in the Sun during His ascension, using "He hath set His tabernacle in the Sun," (Psalm 19:4-5) as their justification.

The Centrality of Christ's Resurrection

Believing that Christ died is no great act of faith—even the Jews, pagans, and unbelievers acknowledge this fact. However, the cornerstone of Christian faith is the resurrection of Christ. Augustine writes, "The resurrection of Christ is the very lock and key of all Christian religion."[13] Scripture makes this clear: "And if Christ be not risen, then is our preaching vain, and your faith is also vain," (1 Corinthians 15:14). "But he said unto them, Be not affrighted: Ye seek Jesus of Nazareth, which was crucified: he is risen; he is not here," (Mark 16:6). "He was seen of Cephas, then of the twelve: after that, he was seen of above five hundred brethren at once," (1 Corinthians 15:4-6). "He seeing this before spake of the resurrection of Christ, that his soul was not left in hell, neither did his flesh see corruption," (Acts 2:31). "So then after the Lord had spoken unto them, he was received up into heaven, and sat on the right hand of God," (Mark 16:19). "Whom the heaven must receive until the times of restitution of all things," (Acts 3:21). "This cup is the new testament in my blood: this do ye, as oft as ye drink it, in remembrance of me. For as often as ye eat this bread, and drink this cup, ye do shew the Lord's death till he come," (1 Corinthians 11:25-26).

Clarification of Christ's Presence

    Objection: "Behold, I am with you always, even unto the end of the world," (Matthew 28:20). Does this not mean that Christ is always physically present?

---

[13] Augustine, *Exposition* on Psalm 120.

Solution: This promise refers to Christ's presence according to His divine nature, grace, and Spirit. As man, Christ is physically absent and remains in Heaven until His return. He Himself affirmed, "For ye have the poor always with you; but me ye have not always," (Matthew 26:11).

Christ's resurrection and ascension demonstrate His victory over death, proving that He is *both* fully God and fully man. His ongoing intercession at the right hand of the Father assures believers of their eternal security and His imminent return in glory.

Chapter 11: Of Predestination

Since the benefits of Christ's death do not extend to all but are applied to a specific chosen number, we must now consider the doctrine of God's Predestination—His decree by which He chooses some to eternal life while rejecting others, leaving them in their sins to be condemned.

Adversaries to the Doctrine of Predestination

1. Pelagians (Old and New): They ridicule and reject this doctrine, asserting that it is unworthy of God to choose some and refuse others, labeling such an act as partial and unjust.

2. Libertines: They abuse this doctrine as an excuse for licentious living, reasoning that if they are predestined, their way of life cannot affect their salvation.

3. Socinians and Arminians: They claim that predestination merely refers to God's foreknowledge of who will believe and obey and who will reject Him. They deny that predestination is independent of human actions.

4. Opponents of Eternal Predestination: These individuals deny that God's decree is eternal, arguing that God only elects people once they believe.

5. Deniers of Certainty: They assert that predestination is changeable, claiming that the elect can become reprobates and vice versa.

6. Papists: They are inconsistent in their teachings. On one hand, they affirm that God chooses freely by His grace. On the other, they claim that God elects based on foreseen good works. Bellarmine, in *De Gratia et Libero Arbitrio*, states that the kingdom of heaven is prepared for those who earn it through their good deeds.

Affirmation of the Doctrine of Predestination

1. There is a Predestination to Life and a Reprobation to Destruction. Scripture attests to this truth: "What if God, willing to shew his wrath, and to make his power known, endured with much longsuffering the vessels of wrath fitted to destruction: and that he might make known the riches of his glory on the vessels of mercy, which he had afore prepared unto glory," (Romans 9:22-23). "And as many as were ordained to eternal life believed," (Acts 13:48). "The Lord hath made all things for himself: yea, even the wicked for the day of evil," (Proverbs 16:4). "For there are certain men crept in unawares, who were before of old ordained to this condemnation," (Jude 4).

Augustine summarizes this in *The City of God*: "There are two societies of men: one predestined to reign with God forever, and the other to suffer eternal punishment with the devil."[14]

---

[14] Augustine, *De Civitate Dei*, Book 15, Chapter 1.

2. Predestination is Eternal. The Scriptures declare that predestination was determined before time began: "For the children being not yet born, neither having done any good or evil, that the purpose of God according to election might stand, not of works, but of him that calleth," (Romans 9:11). "According as he hath chosen us in him before the foundation of the world," (Ephesians 1:4). "Who hath saved us, and called us with an holy calling, not according to our works, but according to his own purpose and grace, which was given us in Christ Jesus before the world began," (2 Timothy 1:9).

3. Predestination is Free and Independent. Election to eternal life is based solely on the will and good pleasure of God, not on foreseen faith or good works. Reprobation, too, is not determined by external causes but by God's sovereign will: "Therefore hath he mercy on whom he will have mercy, and whom he will he hardeneth," (Romans 9:18). "Having predestinated us unto the adoption of children by Jesus Christ to himself, according to the good pleasure of his will," (Ephesians 1:5). "In whom also we have obtained an inheritance, being predestinated according to the purpose of him who worketh all things after the counsel of his own will," (Ephesians 1:11). "Not according to our works, but according to his own purpose and grace," (2 Timothy 1:9).

Augustine affirms, "Faith and obedience are effects of election and cannot be its cause, for they follow after and do not precede it."[15] Scripture further confirms this: "And as many as were ordained to eternal life believed," (Acts 13:48). "We love him, because he first loved us," (1 John 4:19). "For whom he did foreknow, he also did predestinate to be conformed to the image of his Son," (Romans 8:29).

To claim that election is based on foreseen faith or works is to invert the Apostle's words and distort the order of salvation. This is clearly refuted by "Before the children were born or had done any good or evil... Jacob have I loved, but Esau have I hated," (Romans 9:11-12). When asked whether God foresaw their deeds and chose accordingly, the Apostle answers definitively: "That the purpose of God according to election might stand, not of works, but of him that calleth," (Romans 9:12).

4. Predestination is Immutable and Unchangeable. The elect can never perish, nor can the reprobates be saved: "Nevertheless the foundation of God standeth sure, having this seal, The Lord knoweth them that are his," (2 Timothy 2:19). "Rather rejoice, because your names are written in heaven," (Luke 10:20). "He calleth his own sheep by name," (John 10:3). "Who are kept by the power of God through faith unto salvation," (1 Peter 1:5).

---

[15] Augustine, *De Praedestinatione*, Chapter 7.

Those who are predestined will be provided with the means necessary to bring them to glory. If someone who seems holy falls away, it demonstrates not that the elect can fall but that the individual was never truly elect: "They went out from us, but they were not of us; for if they had been of us, they would no doubt have continued with us," (1 John 2:19).

Ambrose declares, "The reason for the distinction is hidden, but the distinction itself is evident."[16] The effect is plain, though the cause remains secret. However, though unknown to us, we trust that it is not unjust, for God's will is righteous and holy. To those who complain, the Apostle responds: "Nay but, O man, who art thou that repliest against God? Shall the thing formed say to him that formed it, Why hast thou made me thus?" (Romans 9:20-21). "O the depth of the riches both of the wisdom and knowledge of God! how unsearchable are his judgments, and his ways past finding out!" (Romans 11:33).

Since all humans are naturally corrupt and undeserving, God shows mercy to one and not to another without *any* injustice. If any are saved, they owe it entirely to God's mercy; if any are condemned, they can only blame their own sin.

Objections and Answers

---

[16] Ambrose, *De Vocatione Gentium*.

Objection: This doctrine encourages licentiousness and despair, undermining efforts toward holiness.

Answer: The proclamation of God's grace for the comfort of believers must not be silenced because the ungodly may twist it. This doctrine provides comfort and assurance to the godly and encourages good works as evidence of our calling and election: "Follow peace with all men, and holiness, without which no man shall see the Lord," (Hebrews 12:14).

Those who are ordained to life will not be slothful but diligent in pursuing good works. Holiness is not the cause of salvation but the way prepared for us to walk in: "For we are his workmanship, created in Christ Jesus unto good works, which God hath before ordained that we should walk in them," (Ephesians 2:10).

No one who trusts in God's appointed means—His Word and sacraments—has any reason to despair.

If you find signs of election in yourself, praise God. If you do not see them in another, pray for them and remain hopeful, for God may yet call them as He called you. Avoid fruitless speculation and focus on making a practical use of this doctrine in humility and faith.

Chapter 12: Of Vocation

"And whom he did predestinate, them he also called;" (Romans 8:30).

God's calling is not only an outward one through the preaching of His holy Word but also an inward, effectual call by the operation of His Holy Spirit. This divine calling works powerfully with the Word to win hearts, making them cling inseparably to Him for salvation.

This calling is the second link in the golden chain of salvation—a link that many adversaries, both ancient and modern, have sought to sever. There are three types of these adversaries:

1. Those Who Condemn the Ministry of the Word: These include the Anabaptists, Gaspar Swenckfeldius, and their followers. They assert that men are called and faith is given, not by means of the Word, but by illumination and the immediate working of the Spirit. Obsessed with speculations and revelations, they claim that God reveals His will to them through dreams and visions. This notion has led to the rise of many impostors, such as Mahomet, Muncer, Simon Magus, Cerinthus, and Montanus. These false teachers misused dreams and visions to spread their monstrous errors. Many of the errors found in Popery, such as the belief in purgatory, originated from supposed visions. Thus, once men stray from the light of

Chapter 12: Of Vocation

God's Word, they easily fall into strange and monstrous delusions.

2. Those Who Undervalue Preaching: This group does not condemn the outward ministry outright but views preaching with disdain, claiming that simply reading the Scriptures is sufficient for salvation. They argue that frequent preaching is unnecessary and even harmful. This view became prevalent among some ministers and their congregations, reinforced by the negligence of many bishops, who abandoned preaching altogether, considering it beneath their dignity. Instead of glorifying their office through faithful preaching, they brought disgrace upon themselves.

3. Patrons of Free Will: These include the Pelagians, Papists, Arminians, and others who seek to uphold human pride by denying the necessity of grace. To support their doctrine of free will, they assert:

1. That the grace of vocation is merely a moral persuasion that inclines the will through the outward preaching of the Word, denying the inward, effectual work of the Spirit.

2. That sufficient grace to believe and be converted is given to all through the Gospel, but the difference between believers and unbelievers lies in their free will.

3. That grace, once received, can be entirely lost, and faith can be cut off.

The Truth of Effectual Calling

1. The Necessity of the Inward Work of the Spirit. The outward preaching of the Word alone cannot create faith or lead a sinner to God without the inward working of the Holy Ghost. Nevertheless, the written Word and its preaching are God's appointed means to bring people to faith in Christ: "Faith cometh by hearing, and hearing by the word of God," (Romans 10:17). "While Peter yet spake these words, the Holy Ghost fell on all them which heard the word," (Acts 10:44). Even Christ Himself took the book of Isaiah and preached the Scripture (Luke 4:16). Philip preached the Scriptures to the Ethiopian eunuch (Acts 8:35). Paul reasoned from the Scriptures (Acts 17:2).

The practice of both Jewish and Christian churches has always been to read and expound the Scriptures for the people's edification (Nehemiah 8:9; Acts 13:15). Timothy is commended for knowing the Scriptures (2 Timothy 3:15). The Word is called the "Word of grace" (Acts 20:32) and the "Word of faith" (Romans 10:8) because it conveys both to us.

In earlier times, God revealed His will through dreams, visions, oracles, and the Urim and Thummim. But now, in these last days, He speaks to us through His Son (Hebrews 1:1). Therefore, as Peter affirms: "We have also a more sure word of prophecy, whereunto ye do well that ye take heed," (2 Peter 1:19).

2. The Importance of Preaching. Though some children, during times of persecution, led their parents

to Christ by reading the Scriptures, bare reading without preaching is insufficient. We cannot expect God's blessing on reading alone when He has provided the means of both reading and preaching. Scripture confirms this: Nehemiah and the Levites not only read the Law but also "gave the sense and caused them to understand," (Nehemiah 8:9). After the reading of the Scriptures, the people desired a "word of exhortation," (Acts 13:15). Christ Himself read from the Scriptures and then preached (Luke 4:16). Without preaching, the Scriptures can be as unintelligible as an unknown tongue (1 Corinthians 14:23).

    3. The Inward and Outward Calling. The grace of vocation is both external and internal:

    1. External: The outward preaching of the Gospel.

    2. Internal: The illumination of the mind, regeneration of the heart, and conversion of the will, turning the heart to God in faith.

    The outward call alone cannot convert; only the inward work of the Spirit can create faith and repentance: "This is the work of God, that ye believe," (John 6:29). "In meekness instructing those that oppose themselves; if God peradventure will give them repentance," (2 Timothy 2:25).

    Human wisdom and arguments cannot change a stony heart; this is God's work: "A new heart also will I give you," (Ezekiel 36:26). "Create in me a clean heart, O

God," (Psalm 51:10). "No man can come to me, except the Father which hath sent me draw him," (John 6:44).

4. Irresistible Grace. The grace of vocation is irresistible because it is grounded in God's purpose and power: "All that the Father giveth me shall come to me," (John 6:37). God does not compel the will with force but draws with cords of love, changing hearts so that they willingly obey.

5. Immutable and Free. God's calling is unchangeable: "The gifts and calling of God are without repentance," (Romans 11:29). Those who are effectually called cannot fall away completely: "I will make an everlasting covenant with them... that they shall not depart from me," (Jeremiah 32:40).

God's calling is entirely free, not based on human merit but solely on His good pleasure: "The wind bloweth where it listeth... so is everyone that is born of the Spirit," (John 3:8).

6. Peculiar to the Elect. Effectual calling is reserved for God's elect: "As many as were ordained to eternal life believed," (Acts 13:48). "Whom he did predestinate, them he also called," (Romans 8:30). Many are called outwardly but not inwardly. Only the elect are called effectually by the Spirit, are justified by grace, and will certainly be glorified. The elect are secure because the links in this golden chain—predestination, calling, justification, and glorification—are bound together by God's unchangeable purpose and invincible power.

Chapter 13: Of Justification

"And whom he called, them he also justified," (Romans 8:30).

We are justified—or accounted righteous—before God, not because of any works or merit of our own, but solely through the merits of Jesus Christ. By faith in Him, our sins are imputed to Christ, and His righteousness is imputed to us.

Adversaries to the Doctrine of Justification
The doctrine of justification faces opposition from various groups:

1. The Anabaptists: They claim that we are justified not by faith alone but also by the cross and affliction.

2. The Papists (Roman Catholics): They deny justification by faith alone and assert that justification comes through faith and works combined, giving greater weight to works. They regard faith not as an instrument of justification but as a virtue that merits or deserves righteousness. They teach that justification is achieved through an inherent righteousness infused into the believer, not by an imputed righteousness.

3. Osiander: He falsely claimed that believers are substantially righteous in Christ in essence as well as in quality, asserting that God imparts His essence into believers, making them a part of Himself.

4. The Familists: This group teaches that each member of their community becomes Christ and that receiving their doctrine constitutes the incarnation.

5. Legalistic Christians: These individuals believe they can be justified by their civil and external righteousness.

6. Libertines: They argue that they can be justified by a "dead" faith without any care for good works.

7. Carnal Professors: These people disregard both faith and works, yet presume they will be saved.

The Papists, by undermining this doctrine, effectively nullify the Gospel and bury Christ again, denying the efficacy of His resurrection for our justification.

The Truth of Justification by Faith

1. Justification by Faith Alone. We are justified without works, by faith alone. This does not mean that faith exists without good works in its essence, but that in the act of justification, faith alone serves as the instrument: "Enter not into judgment with thy servant: for in thy sight shall no man living be justified," (Psalm 143:2). "What is man, that he should be clean?" (Job 15:15). "By the deeds of the law there shall no flesh be justified in his sight," (Romans 3:20). "The just shall live by faith," (Galatians 3:11). "A man is justified by faith without the deeds of the law," (Romans 3:28).

Good works may justify us before men as evidence of our faith, as James states: "Ye see then how that by works a man is justified," (James 2:24). However, before God, we are justified solely by the perfect righteousness of Christ, which is applied to us by faith.

2. Faith as the Instrument of Justification. Faith is not the cause of justification but the instrument by which we receive Christ's righteousness. It is not our faith's merit that justifies us but Christ's merit: "The righteousness of God which is by faith of Jesus Christ unto all and upon all them that believe," (Romans 3:22). "Being justified freely by his grace through the redemption that is in Christ Jesus," (Romans 3:24). "That I may be found in him, not having mine own righteousness... but that which is through the faith of Christ," (Philippians 3:9).

3. Types of Righteousness. There are three types of righteousness:

1. Glorifying Righteousness: Perfect and inherent in the world to come.

2. Sanctifying Righteousness: Inherent but imperfect in this life.

3. Justifying Righteousness: Perfect but not inherent—imputed to us through Christ.

The righteousness by which we are justified is not infused into us but imputed to us: "Abraham believed God, and it was counted unto him for righteousness," (Romans 4:5). "We are made the righteousness of God in him," (2 Corinthians 5:21).

Augustine affirms: "We are made righteous in Him, not by our own righteousness but by His."[17]

4. The Nature of Justifying Faith
When we say that we are justified by faith alone, we do not mean a solitary or dead faith without works, but a living, active faith: "Faith... worketh by love," (Galatians 5:6).

Faith excludes works only in the act of justification, not from the nature of faith itself.

The Components of Justification
    1. Imputation of Christ's Righteousness: We are counted righteous because Christ's righteousness is imputed to us.
    2. Forgiveness of Sins: Our sins are forgiven through the merits of Christ.
    The inward cause of our justification is God's mercy; the outward cause is Christ's merit. The formal cause is the imputation of Christ's righteousness, and the instrumental cause is faith, apart from works. Thus, good works are excluded from the act of justification but not from the life of faith.

---

[17] Augustine, *Enchiridion*, Chapter 41.

Chapter 14: Of Sanctification

"Whom he justified, them he also glorified," (Romans 8:30).

The glorification of believers, which will be completed in the life to come, begins in this life through sanctification. Sanctification is both a change in our condition, as we are made partakers of spiritual blessings, and a change in our nature, as we are renewed in righteousness and true holiness according to the image of God.

Adversaries to the Doctrine of Sanctification

Several groups have opposed this truth: 1. Simon Magus and his followers: They taught that sin defiles only the body, not the soul, granting license to all forms of immorality. Modern libertines follow this pattern, scoffing at the call to holy living.

2. Anabaptist sects, such as the Adamites and Familists: These groups claim that they are perfect and entirely free from sin, asserting that they live as purely as Christ Himself. Similar beliefs were held by the Pelagians, Donatists, and later the Fraticelli, who taught that those who achieve such perfection no longer need prayer, fasting, or any exercise of piety.

3. Certain Protestants: In opposition to the Roman Catholic insistence on an inherent righteousness that justifies, these individuals deny any inherent grace

in believers, teaching instead that all spiritual graces exist solely in Christ and not in us.

The Call to Holiness

Having been justified by faith through God's grace, believers are called to pursue holiness:

1. To glorify God's name: "Ye are bought with a price: therefore glorify God in your body and in your spirit, which are God's," (1 Corinthians 6:20).

2. To fulfill God's will: "For this is the will of God, even your sanctification," (1 Thessalonians 4:3).

3. To fulfill the purpose of our election: "He hath chosen us in him before the foundation of the world, that we should be holy," (Ephesians 1:4).

4. To fulfill the purpose of our redemption: "That we being delivered out of the hand of our enemies might serve him without fear, in holiness and righteousness," (Luke 1:74).

5. To fulfill the purpose of our calling: "For God hath not called us unto uncleanness, but unto holiness," (1 Thessalonians 4:7). "Without holiness, no man shall see the Lord," (Hebrews 12:14).

The Imperfection of Sanctification

While believers must pursue holiness, they cannot achieve sinless perfection in this life: "If we say that we have no sin, we deceive ourselves, and the truth is not in us," (1 John 1:8). "In many things we offend all," (James 3:2). "There is no man that sinneth not," (1 Kings

8:46). "Who can say, I have made my heart clean, I am pure from my sin?" (Proverbs 20:9). "There is not a just man upon earth, that doeth good, and sinneth not," (Ecclesiastes 7:20).

The examples of godly men confirm this truth: Noah became drunk (Genesis 9:21), Abraham lied (Genesis 20:2), Lot fell into grievous sin (Genesis 19:33), David committed adultery (2 Samuel 11), Peter denied Christ (Matthew 26:69-75), and Paul confessed his internal struggle with sin (Romans 7:23-24). "Be ye therefore perfect, even as your Father which is in heaven is perfect," (Matthew 5:48). This verse presents God's holiness as a model to strive toward, not a standard we can fully attain. "Whosoever is born of God doth not commit sin," (1 John 3:9). This refers to sin's dominion and habitual practice, not to absolute sinlessness. Believers still sin due to weakness, but they do not return to sin as their master.

The Nature of Sanctification

1. Inherent in Believers: The righteousness by which we are justified is imputed to us in Christ; the righteousness by which we are sanctified is infused into us by the Holy Spirit.

2. Ongoing and Progressive: Sanctification frees us from the pollution of sin through a gradual renewal: "The inward man is renewed day by day," (2 Corinthians 4:16). "Stir up the gift of God, which is in thee," (2 Timothy 1:6). "Add to your faith virtue... for if these

things be in you and abound, they make you fruitful," (2 Peter 1:5-8).

Evidence of Sanctification

Sanctification serves as proof of justification: "There is therefore now no condemnation to them which are in Christ Jesus, who walk not after the flesh, but after the Spirit," (Romans 8:1). "In this the children of God are manifest, and the children of the devil," (1 John 3:10). "They that are Christ's have crucified the flesh with the affections and lusts," (Galatians 5:24).

God's Awareness of Sin in His Saints

God does not overlook sin in believers: David was rebuked for his sin by the prophet Nathan (2 Samuel 12:7-10). David himself acknowledged his sin and prayed for forgiveness: "Have mercy upon me, O God... blot out my transgressions," (Psalm 51:1). Jesus teaches His disciples to pray for forgiveness: "Forgive us our debts," (Matthew 6:12). Peter wept bitterly after denying Christ (Matthew 26:75).

Believers must mourn over their sins and continually renew their souls through repentance, knowing that God's grace sustains their sanctification.

Chapter 15: Of the Moral Law

Christ has delivered believers from the condemnation and curse of the Law, but not from the obligation to obey it. The Moral Law remains a rule of life for Christians. Some oppose this truth by misinterpreting passages such as "Ye are not under the law, but under grace," (Romans 6:14) and "The law is not made for a righteous man," (1 Timothy 1:9). These adversaries, often called *Antinomians*, teach:

1. The Moral Law should be excluded entirely from the Church.

2. Believers' consciences should no longer be troubled or convicted by the preaching of the Law but instead comforted solely by the grace of Christ.

3. The Law and Christ are incompatible, with one negating the other.

4. The Law has no use for a believer and is unnecessary as a guide for life.

Christ's Fulfillment of the Law

Christ is the fulfillment of the Law, but not its destruction. As Augustine wrote, Christ is "the perfecting end, not the consuming end." Jesus Himself declared, "Think not that I am come to destroy the law, or the prophets: I am not come to destroy, but to fulfil," (Matthew 5:17). He further warned, "Whosoever shall break one of these least commandments, and shall teach men so, he shall be called the least in the kingdom of heaven," (Matthew 5:19). The Apostle Paul reaffirmed this: "Do we then make void the law through faith? God forbid: yea, we establish the law," (Romans 3:31).

The Believer's Relationship to the Law

Although believers are not under the Law as a means of condemnation or as a tyrant, they are still called to obey it as children obey a loving Father. Believers are freed from the Law's penalty but not from the call to obedience. Their obedience is motivated by love and joy, not fear: "This is the love of God, that we keep his commandments: and his commandments are not grievous," (1 John 5:3).

Through the Spirit's work in their hearts, the Law becomes a "law of liberty" (James 1:25), not a burden.

The Twofold Use of the Law

1. Civil Use: The Law restrains sin and maintains order in society.

2. Spiritual Use: The Law reveals sin and drives people to Christ. Luther wrote that the Law serves as a mirror, showing our sinfulness and need for grace. The Apostle Paul explained: "I had not known sin, but by the law," (Romans 7:7).

The Law humbles us, exposing our spiritual blindness and corruption. It leads us to renounce self-righteousness and cling to Christ. As Paul wrote, "The law was our schoolmaster to bring us unto Christ,"

(Galatians 3:24). Christ is the "end of the law for righteousness to every one that believeth," (Romans 10:4). He fulfilled the Law perfectly, attaining the righteousness that believers cannot achieve on their own.

The Law's Continuing Role

Once the Law has brought a person to Christ, its condemning power ceases, but its guiding power remains. The believer follows the Law: Not to earn righteousness: Our justification is through Christ alone. To express gratitude to God: "We love him, because he first loved us," (1 John 4:19). To glorify God and edify others: Our obedience serves as a testimony to the watching world: "Let your light so shine before men, that they may see your good works, and glorify your Father which is in heaven," (Matthew 5:16).

The believer's observance of the Law, therefore, is an act of worship and a means of demonstrating faithfulness to God, not a means of earning salvation.

Chapter 16: Of Good Works

Although we are justified freely by the grace of God through the redemption that is in Jesus Christ (Romans 3:24), we are still commanded to maintain good works:

1. Out of thankfulness to God for such a great benefit and to glorify His name.
2. To assure ourselves of the truth of our faith by the fruits it produces.
3. To edify, win, and encourage others by our good example.

Adversaries to Good Works

1. The Papists — They claim that good works are meritorious and contribute to salvation, thus overvaluing them.
2. The Libertines — They undervalue good works, believing them to be opposed to faith. They interpret Christian liberty as freedom from the obligation to live righteously and think they may live as they please.

The Scriptural Command for Good Works

The following passages affirm the necessity of good works: "We are created in Christ Jesus unto good works, which God hath before ordained that we should walk in them," (Ephesians 2:10). "[Christ] gave Himself for us, that He might redeem us from all iniquity and purify unto Himself a peculiar people, zealous of good works," (Titus 2:14). "We must all appear before the judgment seat of Christ, that every one may receive the things done in his body, according to that he hath done, whether it be good or bad," (2 Corinthians 5:10). "I saw the dead, small and great, stand before God; and the books were opened... and the dead were judged out of those things which were written in the books, according to their works," (Revelation 20:12). We are admonished to "have our conversation honest among the Gentiles," (1 Peter 2:12) and to "be careful to maintain good works," (Titus 3:8).

The Imperfection of Our Works

Our best works do not merit anything from God because:

1. They are imperfect: "All our righteousnesses are as filthy rags," (Isaiah 64:6).

2. They are a debt we owe to God: Jesus taught, "When ye shall have done all those things which are commanded you, say, 'We are unprofitable servants: we have done that which was our duty to do,'" (Luke 17:10).

3. They are God's work in us: "It is God which worketh in you both to will and to do of his good pleasure," (Philippians 2:13). Jesus said, "Without me ye can do nothing," (John 15:5).

4. They cannot replace the merits of Christ: To claim merit for our works undermines Christ's death

and makes His sacrifice appear unnecessary or insufficient.

The Reward of Good Works Objection: Eternal life is called a reward: "[*God*] will render to every man according to his deeds," (Romans 2:6); "Behold, I come quickly, and my reward is with me, to give every man according as his work shall be," (Revelation 22:12). Solution: There is a difference between a reward of debt and a reward of grace. Paul distinguishes this in Romans 4:4, stating that a reward given out of grace is not owed but freely given. Eternal life is a reward of grace, not earned by works but promised by God's mercy. Augustine wrote, "When God crowns our works, He is crowning His own gifts."[18]

The Apostle Paul described eternal life as "the gift of God," (Romans 6:23), contrasting it with the wages of sin, which are death. The Kingdom of Heaven is referred to as "the inheritance of the saints," (Colossians 1:12) rather than the wages of laborers. In Jesus' parable of the laborers (Matthew 20), all received the same wages regardless of their hours worked, illustrating that the reward is a gift of grace, not a payment owed for service.

Good works are necessary not for justification, but as evidence of our salvation, a means of glorifying God, and a testimony to others. We perform good works

---

[18] *Enarr.* in Psalm 102.

not to earn righteousness but to reflect the grace that has been freely given to us in Christ.

Chapter 17: Of Death and Burial

There is no living person who will escape death, for life is a journey that inevitably comes to an end. When we complete our course here, our body returns to dust in the earth, and our soul returns to God who gave it (Ecclesiastes 12:7).

Adversaries to the Doctrine of Death and Burial

1. The Nazarens — An early heretical group who taught that the souls of humans and animals shared the same nature and substance.

2. The Arabici — A sect in Arabia who falsely claimed that the soul dies along with the body, just as an animal's soul perishes.

3. Soul Sleep Advocates — Those who asserted that while the soul does not die, it remains in a state of sleep in the grave until the day of judgment.

4. Materialists — Modern individuals who argue that humanity is wholly mortal and that the soul perishes at death. This belief has been perpetuated in certain books asserting the soul's mortality.

5. Pope John XXIII — He held the erroneous belief that the soul does not see God until the day of judgment.

6. Familists — A sect that claimed burial was unnecessary, misinterpreting Christ's words, "Let the dead bury their dead," (Luke 9:60).

7. Irreverent Persons — Those who, while not heretical, show inhumanity by exposing the dead to indecent and irreverent treatment.

8. The Papists — They regard the burial of the dead as a meritorious work, drawing this belief from the Apocryphal book of Tobit.

Scriptural Truths About Death and Burial

The Scriptures refute these errors: "The dust shall return to the earth as it was, and the spirit shall return to God who gave it," (Ecclesiastes 12:7). "Lord Jesus, receive my spirit," (Acts 7:59). "This day shalt thou be with me in Paradise," (Luke 23:43).

When the Sadducees questioned Christ about the resurrection, He answered, "God is not the God of the dead, but of the living," (Matthew 22:32), silencing their objections.

The Hope of the Soul's Journey After Death

The fears and terrors of the wicked at their death and the hopes and exceeding joy of the godly at their departure bear witness to the truth that the soul does not sleep but immediately enters into joy or sorrow. The soul has a divine instinct or assurance of this reality.

Christian Burial

After the soul departs, the body should be laid to rest in a decent and respectful burial:

1. A Testament to Human Dignity: Burial honors the shared nature of humanity and acknowledges the frailty to which all are subject.

2. Scriptural Examples: The patriarchs were diligent in arranging their burial places (Genesis 23:19; 50:25), and the Jewish people treated burial with care as a demonstration of faith in the resurrection.

3. A Simpler Practice in Early Christianity: As doctrine became clearer, fewer ceremonies were used. For example, Tabitha's body was simply washed before burial (Acts 9:37).

Condemnation of Superstition

We reject the numerous superstitious and impious ceremonies that the Papists have added to Christian burials. However, we must still regard the bodies of our Christian friends as precious, for they:

1. Were Members of Christ: "Know ye not that your bodies are the members of Christ?" (1 Corinthians 6:15).

2. Were Temples of the Holy Ghost: "Your body is the temple of the Holy Ghost," (1 Corinthians 6:19).

3. Will Be Raised Glorious: On the last day, they will be raised and transformed to be like Christ's glorious body (Philippians 3:21).

The Purpose of Burial

While burial does not matter to the deceased, it serves vital purposes:

Chapter 17: Of Death and Burial

1. To Honor Human Nature: It demonstrates respect for the sanctity of human life.

2. To Comfort the Bereaved: It provides solace to surviving family and friends.

3. To Instruct the Living: Funerals remind the living of their mortality and encourage reflection on eternal matters.

In this way, Christian burial is not an empty ritual but a testimony of faith in the resurrection and the promise of life everlasting.

Chapter 18: Of the Resurrection

Although our bodies, when we die, will return to dust and ashes, they shall at the last day be raised again, reunited with our souls, and together will enter into either everlasting joy or eternal sorrow.

Adversaries to the Doctrine of Resurrection

1. The Sadducees — They denied the resurrection entirely, but they were rebuked and silenced by Christ (Matthew 22:23–32).

2. Hymenaeus and Philetus — They taught false doctrines about the resurrection, leading many astray with their corrupt teachings (2 Timothy 2:17).

3. Simon Magus and Menander — Early heretics who spread dangerous errors.

4. The Familists and Modern Fanatics — These groups reject the literal resurrection of the body and claim that the resurrection refers only to a rising from sin or a mystical body of believers. They assert that the physical body will be annihilated and cease to exist.

5. The Manichees — They believed in a Pythagorean transmigration of souls, imagining that souls pass into new bodies after death.

6. The Anabaptists — They claimed that while there will be a resurrection, it will be with entirely new and different bodies rather than the same ones we have now.

Chapter 18: Of the Resurrection

Scriptural Evidence for the Resurrection

The Scriptures refute these false teachings: "If in this life only we have hope in Christ, we are of all men most miserable," (1 Corinthians 15:19). "Why stand we in jeopardy every hour?" (1 Corinthians 15:30). "The hour is coming in which all that are in the graves shall hear His voice," (John 5:28). "The trumpet shall sound, and the dead shall be raised incorruptible," (1 Corinthians 15:52). "The sea gave up the dead which were in it, and death and the grave delivered up the dead which were in them," (Revelation 20:13). "We must all appear before the judgment seat of Christ, that every one may receive the things done in his body," (2 Corinthians 5:10). "Though after my skin worms destroy this body, yet in my flesh shall I see God, whom I shall see for myself, and mine eyes shall behold, and not another," (Job 19:26–27).

The Importance of the Resurrection

The resurrection of the body is a cornerstone of the Christian faith, as affirmed by Paul: "If Christ be not risen, then is our preaching vain, and your faith is also vain," (1 Corinthians 15:14).

Belief in the resurrection shapes how we live and view our mortality. It serves as a hope for the godly and a solemn reminder of accountability for the ungodly.

This doctrine assures believers that though their bodies rest in the grave, they will rise again, transformed and glorified, to eternal life with Christ.

Chapter 19:
Of Glorification in Heaven

"And whom He justified, them He also glorified." After the resurrection and the final judgment, the saints—God's chosen—shall enter into eternal triumph with Christ and reign with Him forever.

Adversaries to the Doctrine of Glorification

1. Cerinthus — He falsely claimed, under the guise of angelic revelation, that after the resurrection, Christ would establish a 1,000-year reign on earth where the saints would indulge in worldly pleasures.

2. Mohammedans — The Quran, influenced by Cerinthus' ideas, promises a carnal paradise filled with earthly delights.

3. The Anabaptists and Other Groups — They expect a temporary earthly kingdom where the righteous alone will inherit the earth after the destruction of the wicked.

4. The Familists — They teach that the joys of heaven are fully experienced in this world and deny a separate heavenly glorification.

Scriptural Evidence for Heavenly Glorification

"Then we which are alive and remain shall be caught up together with them in the clouds, to meet the Lord in the air: and so shall we ever be with the Lord," (1 Thessalonians 4:17). This clearly indicates that after death, the saints will be taken to be with Christ, not left on earth. "When this earthly tabernacle is dissolved, we have a building of God, a house not made with hands, eternal in the heavens," (2 Corinthians 5:1). "An inheritance incorruptible and undefiled, reserved in heaven for you," (1 Peter 1:4). "Henceforth there is laid up for me a crown of righteousness," (2 Timothy 4:8). "Eye hath not seen, nor ear heard, neither have entered into the heart of man, the things which God hath prepared for them that love Him," (1 Corinthians 2:9). "Our vile body shall be changed, that it may be fashioned like unto His glorious body," (Philippians 3:20-21). "They that be wise shall shine as the brightness of the firmament, and they that turn many to righteousness as the stars forever and ever," (Daniel 12:3). "And they shall reign forever and ever," (Revelation 22:5).

Interpretation of the 1,000 Years (Revelation 20)

The 1,000 years mentioned in Revelation 20 are not to be taken as a literal earthly reign of the saints but refer symbolically to the condition of the Church in this present age, during which Satan is bound and cannot deceive the nations as he once did. The ultimate glorification occurs in heaven, where the redeemed will dwell with Christ eternally, free from sin and sorrow, crowned with everlasting joy.

Chapter 20: Of Hell

The reprobates, the wicked, and ungodly men, after receiving their dreadful sentence, shall be cast into the everlasting torment of hellfire, prepared for the devil and his angels.

Adversaries to the Doctrine of Hell

1. Deniers of Hell and the Devil — Some claim there is no literal devil or hell, asserting that "the devil" is merely a metaphor for human sinful desires and that "hell" refers only to an evil conscience.

2. Postponers of Hell — Others acknowledge the existence of hell but argue that its torments do not begin until the day of judgment.

3. Universal Salvation Advocates — Some teach that the torments of hell are not eternal and that even the damned and devils will ultimately be saved. This belief was propagated by an ancient sect known as the *Liberatores* and is embraced by some Muslims who believe that those in hell may be released upon calling for mercy.

Scriptural Evidence for Hell's Reality and Eternity

"God spared not the angels that sinned, but cast them down to hell, and delivered them into chains of darkness," (2 Peter 2:4). "The angels which kept not their first estate... he hath reserved in everlasting chains under darkness," (Jude 6). "They shall be punished with everlasting destruction," (2 Thessalonians 1:9). "Where their worm dieth not, and the fire is not quenched," (Mark 9:44). "The devil that deceived them was cast into the lake of fire and brimstone... and shall be tormented day and night forever and ever," (Revelation 20:10). "Depart from me, ye cursed, into everlasting fire, prepared for the devil and his angels," (Matthew 25:41). "Between us and you there is a great gulf fixed, so that they which would pass from hence to you cannot; neither can they pass to us," (Luke 16:26).

Refutation of Erroneous Beliefs Against the Denial of Hell and the Devil

The scriptures consistently affirm the existence of Satan and a place of judgment prepared for him and his followers. Against the Postponement of Hell: The fallen angels were cast into hell immediately after their rebellion (2 Peter 2:4), demonstrating that hell's torments are not confined to the final judgment. Against Universal Salvation: Hell's punishments are explicitly described as everlasting. "Their fire never shall be quenched," (Mark 9:44), and "the smoke of their torment ascendeth up forever and ever," (Revelation 14:11).

"Oh that they were wise, that they understood this, that they would consider their latter end!" (Deuteronomy 32:29). Let these truths move every soul to repentance and humility before the God of justice and mercy. The great gulf between heaven and hell is fixed, and there is no crossing from torment to peace after death. Now is the time to seek salvation and flee from the wrath to come.

Chapter 21: Of Purgatory

There is no third or middle place between heaven and hell where the souls of the departed go. Therefore, the doctrine of purgatory, along with all its associated practices—such as pardons, prayers for the dead, and masses—is not only unfounded and unbiblical but also rooted in heathen traditions and is blasphemous.

Origins and Proponents of the Doctrine of Purgatory

1. Heathen Origin: The belief in an intermediate place for purging souls was first propagated by pagan philosophies.

2. Heretical Influence: It was introduced among Christians by early heretics such as Simon Magus and Montanus.

3. Roman Church's Adoption: The Roman Catholic Church adopted purgatory due to the financial gain it provided. By capitalizing on the fears of the laity, the clergy enriched themselves through indulgences, masses, and pardons for the souls they claimed to be suffering.

Description of Purgatory According to Its Advocates Location: Supposedly situated next to hell. Nature of Pain: Some claim its suffering is akin to hellfire, though others attempt to soften the severity. Duration: Allegedly, souls remain there until the final judgment unless released earlier through prayers and payments.

King Henry IV of France resolved this doubt in a memorable jest. When asked to pay for masses to deliver a soul from purgatory, he quipped that if the soul was truly released, it should take care not to return there again! Such wit exposed the fraudulent nature of this doctrine.

Scriptural Rebuttal

1. Only Two Destinations: Scripture consistently presents only two destinations for souls—heaven or hell: "Wide is the gate, and broad is the way, that leadeth to destruction... Strait is the gate, and narrow is the way, which leadeth unto life," (Matthew 7:13-14).

2. Immediate Judgment: "The dust shall return to the earth as it was, and the spirit shall return unto God who gave it," (Ecclesiastes 12:7).

3. No Intermediate State: When Christ taught about the rich man and Lazarus (Luke 16:26), He emphasized the finality of their conditions: "Between us and you there is a great gulf fixed."

Refuting the Papal Claims

The claims of purgatory are inconsistent and unsupported, even within the Roman Church: The location, type of suffering, and duration of purgatory have no consensus. The idea that the Pope can release souls from purgatory for a price exposes the practice as mercenary.

Chapter 21: Of Purgatory

Purgatory is a fabrication born out of superstition and greed. If purgatory does not exist, then indulgences, prayers for the dead, and paid masses are useless. True salvation is secured through Christ alone, not by the rites or intercessions of men. The attempt to purge souls with money mocks God's grace and justice. May the faithful turn away from such deceptions and cling to the truth of God's Word, which proclaims: "If the Son therefore shall make you free, ye shall be free indeed," (John 8:36).

Chapter 22: Of Images

The worship of images, relics, the cross, and similar objects is not only vain, unwarranted, and contrary to God's Word but also constitutes heathenish and abominable idolatry.

Adversaries and Their Beliefs

1. The Roman Catholics: The Roman Catholic Church not only erects and venerates images but also condemns as heretics those who refuse to do likewise.

2. Pseudo-Lutherans: These groups retain images in their churches, claiming they serve as "laymen's books" to edify believers and remind them of heavenly things, though they deny worshipping the images.

3. Historical Practices: When Constantinople was sacked, the Turks refrained from destroying Christian icons and images outright but defaced them by gouging out the eyes—showing their disdain for idolatry without complete destruction.

Testimonies from History

The ancient Romans initially prohibited images, considering it sacrilege to represent heavenly things with earthly forms, as they believed true understanding of God could only be attained mentally. The Jews and early Christians strictly forbade images in their places of worship, guarding against any form of idolatry.

Chapter 22: Of Images

The Papist Excuse for Images

The Roman Catholic defense is that they do not worship the image itself but rather the deity or saint represented by the image. However, this argument mirrors the rationale used by ancient heathens, as recorded by Plutarch, who noted that idolaters believed they were venerating the divine essence rather than the physical statue.

Biblical condemnation of Image Worship.

God forbade not only the worship of graven images but also the worship of Himself through an image (Deuteronomy 4:15-16). Creating an image of God assigns Him a bodily form He does not possess, leading to theological error or heresy.

The Saints and Angels Saints' images are not to be worshipped because the saints themselves are not to be worshipped. The worship of angels is expressly forbidden (Colossians 2:18), and the angels themselves reject it (Revelation 19:10, 22:9), reminding us they are fellow servants.

The True Representation of Christ

The most faithful representation of Christ is found in Scripture: "Before your eyes Jesus Christ hath been evidently set forth, crucified among you," (Galatians 3:1). A crucifix or painted image cannot communicate the depth of Christ's passion and salvation. Instead, we see the living representation of

Christ in the holy Scriptures, in the sacrament of the Lord's Supper, and in acts of charity to our brothers and sisters.

The Dangers of Images in Worship

Even when not worshipped, images in places of worship can distract the mind and lead it away from true spiritual reflection. Augustine warned against this, stating that the practice of using images in worship is "an invention of diabolical deception."[19]

Conclusion

The use of images in worship is not a harmless practice but a dangerous gateway to idolatry. God calls His people to worship Him in spirit and truth, not through physical representations. The living Word, the sacraments, and the example of Christ's love in action serve as the true "images" that draw believers closer to Him. Let all believers heed the command to shun idolatry and cling to the pure worship that exalts God alone.

---

[19] Augustine, *Enarrationes* in Psalmos 113.

Chapter 23: Of the Church

The Church is the body of Christ, comprising the whole company of God's elect, called and gathered by His holy Word and Spirit out of all mankind, from the beginning to the end of the world, into one fellowship with Christ and communion with one another. Although many are called, but few are chosen, many are joined unto the Church who are not truly united to Christ. They may hold outward communion with the saints without having any inward fellowship with the Son of God. Nevertheless, we are to regard all who are outwardly called and profess the true faith as members of the true Church until the Lord—the searcher of all hearts, who alone knows who are His—reveals the truth at His appearing on the great day.

Adversaries to this Truth

1. The Seekers: Deny that there is any true Church upon earth.
2. Anabaptists, Familists, Brownists, and Separatists: Insist that the visible Church must be free of all sin and sinners.
3. Roman Catholics: Claim that the true Catholic Church is a mixed company of both the righteous and the wicked.
4. Papist Doctrine: Exalt the Pope as the head of the Church, bringing great reproach upon Christ.

5. To support their system, Papists maintain three critical errors: That the Church cannot err. That the Church is always visible. That the Word and sacraments are insufficient marks of the true Church.

6. Anabaptists: Misuse the doctrine of the communion of saints to support the idea of communal property and the abolishment of private possessions in the civil state.

The Meaning of the Word "Church"

The term *Church* (from the German *Kirche*) is commonly understood to mean "God's house" or the place of divine worship. The word likely derives from the Greek *kuriakon* ("the Lord's [*house*]"). The material temple is referred to as God's house in John 2:16 and Matthew 23:21, and believers themselves are also referred to as God's house (1 Peter 2:5; Ephesians 2:22).

However, in the New Testament, the word *ecclesia* signifies "the congregation" or "assembly of saints" and is often translated as "Church" (1 Corinthians 11:18, 22). While the word can refer to the meeting place, its primary meaning pertains to the people gathered in worship. Therefore, it is wrong to make a great fuss over the term and derisively call places of worship "steeplehouses."

The Continuity of the Church

There has always been a Church upon the earth: From Adam through Abel, Seth, Enoch, and Noah, and in their families until Abraham. In Abraham's descendants until Christ's coming. With the coming of Christ, the Church's walls were expanded to include the Gentiles (Matthew 28:19; Acts 2:47).

In the days of the apostles: Churches were gathered and confirmed (Revelation 2–3). Ministers were set apart for the work of ministry (Acts 11, 13). These ministers were given authority to ordain others (Titus 1:5).

This succession has continued through all ages and remains today. Wherever the same Gospel is preached, the same sacraments are duly administered, believers profess the same faith, and submit to the same ordinances—as is the case in England and Scotland—there is a true Church of Christ, as there was in the time of the apostles.

The True Catholic Church

The true Catholic Church is the company of God's elect alone: "Christ gave Himself for it," (Ephesians 5:25). It is "the Church of the firstborn, whose names are written in heaven," (Hebrews 12:22). It is "the body of Christ," (Colossians 1:18) and "the household of God," (Ephesians 2:19). Within this Church, there is no condemnation (Romans 8:1), and outside of it, there is no salvation.

Hypocrites and the wicked are not members of this true Church, for "what fellowship has Christ with

Belial?" (2 Corinthians 6:16). This Church is both: Invisible: Its members' faith and inward union with Christ are unseen. Invincible: "The gates of hell shall not prevail against it," (Matthew 16:18).

The Visible and Invisible Church

Many are in the Church who are not truly of it, being outwardly called but not inwardly renewed. This distinction forms the doctrine of the visible and invisible Church: Invisible Church: Composed of the elect alone, called invisible because their faith and true spiritual union with Christ are not visible. Visible Church: Consists of all who outwardly profess the faith and join in public worship.

The foundation for this distinction is laid by Christ Himself (Matthew 20:16). The parable of the tares (Matthew 13) teaches that hypocrites and sinners may exist within the visible Church. However, this does not invalidate the Church or justify separation from it, as some claim. Instead, we are to continue recognizing it as a true Church for the sake of the elect within it. Even St. Paul referred to the Church at Corinth as "a Church of God" despite the presence of heretics, fornicators, and other sinners among them.

Christ as the Head of the Church

As the body of Christ, the Church has one head—Christ alone: "He is the head of the body, the Church," (Colossians 1:18; Ephesians 5:23). No one else can serve as head because only Christ can impart life, grace, and spiritual nourishment.

The Pope cannot be the head of the Church:

1. Not a temporal or secular head: The Church is not a kingdom of this world (John 18:36).

2. Not a spiritual head: The Pope cannot give spiritual life and grace to the Church.

3. Not a ministerial head: He cannot administer the Word and sacraments to every Church in the world, nor does he do so even within his own jurisdiction. His supposed headship is unjustified, as it rests solely on the ministry he cannot faithfully discharge.

The Pope also cannot be the *Lieutenant General* or *Vicar of Christ*, for a lieutenant presumes the absence of the one he represents. Yet Christ has promised, "Lo, I am with you always," (Matthew 28:20), confirming His perpetual presence in His Church. Therefore, there is no place for the Pope's claimed vicarage.

The Church Is Not Free from Error

The Churches of Asia and Judea, which have fallen and are no longer true Churches, testify that no Church on earth is free from error. This includes the Church of Rome, which is led by the Pope—a mere man who is susceptible to error. The Pope, described as "the man of sin," (2 Thessalonians 2:3), cannot help but err. Historical records from their own writers bear witness that many Popes have been guilty of grievous sins, including necromancy, blasphemy, heresy, and immorality. These Popes have denied Christ, persecuted His Church, mocked His truth, and turned His holy ordinances into profane mockeries. Therefore, the Church of Rome can no longer hide its abominations under a false claim of infallibility.

Even though Christ has always preserved a visible Church on earth where believers publicly profess the common faith, it is possible for the Church to be hidden from view due to persecution, as in the days of Elijah (1 Kings 19:10). When asked by the Papists where the true Church was before the Reformation of Luther and Calvin, the answer is that it was in the wilderness (Revelation 12:6). Despite the dark times of Popery, the flames of persecution revealed where Christ's true sheep were, distinguishing them from the wolves.

The marks of the true Church are the same as they were in the beginning:

1. The preaching of the Word of God.

2. The administration of the sacraments.

In contrast, the marks claimed by the Roman Church—such as antiquity, large numbers, and miracles—are unreliable. The synagogue of Satan has existed since the beginning, and Christ's true Church is often described as a "little flock" (Luke 12:32) rather than a vast multitude. The signs of Antichrist include lying wonders designed to deceive (2 Thessalonians 2:9).

The Spiritual Communion of Saints

Chapter 23: Of the Church

The Church is a spiritual commonwealth, and the communion of saints is spiritual rather than temporal. It does not entail abolishing private possessions or enforcing communal ownership of all goods.

Objection: Acts 4:32 says that the early Christians had all things in common.

Solution: Acts 5:4 clarifies that private ownership remained intact: "While it remained, was it not your own? And after it was sold, was it not in your own power?" The early Church practiced voluntary generosity for the relief of the poor, not mandatory surrender of all possessions. If everything had been held in common, there would be no need for exhortations to generosity, no reason for Paul to labor with his own hands, and no risk of becoming a burden to others.

The Catholic and Particular Church

The Church is one, as there is only one faith (Ephesians 4:5). However, it is distinguished as: The Catholic (Universal) Church: Comprising believers from all times and places. Particular Churches: Local assemblies identified by their specific locations (e.g., the Church at Corinth).

The Roman Church falsely claims the title of "Catholic." In reality, it is a particular, heretical Church that is neither universal nor orthodox. Those who refer to Romanists as "Catholics" are mistaken, as they do not profess the true faith of the universal Church. Their religion is not the ancient faith but a new and corrupt system, composed of human inventions with no basis in Scripture.

Chapter 24: Of the Sacraments

The sacraments are holy and visible signs and seals ordained by God to more fully declare and assure us of the promises of the Gospel. The sacraments of the New Testament are only two: Baptism and the Lord's Supper.

Adversaries to This Doctrine

1. Heretics (both ancient and modern): Deny the necessity or existence of any sacraments, claiming they are useless in the Church.

2. Anabaptists: Argue that the sacraments serve only as outward badges of Christian profession, with no further spiritual significance.

3. Roman Catholics: Assert that sacraments confer grace by the very act of performing them (*ex opere operato*) and declare that there are seven sacraments of the New Testament, condemning those who affirm fewer or deny that they are true sacraments instituted by Christ.

The Institution of the Sacraments

Although the term *sacrament* does not appear in Scripture, the equivalent term *mystery* is found, and the ordinances themselves were instituted by Christ:

Baptism: "Go ye therefore, and teach all nations, baptizing them..." (Matthew 28:19). The Lord's Supper: "He took bread... saying, 'This do in remembrance of Me,'" (Luke 22:19-20).

The sacraments are not mere symbols but also seals and pledges that confirm the promises given in God's Word. The Apostle Paul calls circumcision "a seal of the righteousness of faith," (Romans 4:11). However, this does not imply that the sacraments add strength to the promise, as though it were weak, but rather that they confirm and assure us of it.

Sacraments as Means of Grace

Although sacraments do not *confer* grace by their own power, they are *means* by which grace is conveyed. Since they employ visible, tangible elements that engage the senses, they serve as conduits to bring the spiritual truths they signify to our understanding. Yet this is accomplished not by the act of administration itself or the repetition of specific words, but by the power of God's ordinance and the operation of the Holy Spirit.

If the sacraments contained grace within themselves—as medicine in a container—it would follow that grace is always conferred by the outward act alone. However, Scripture shows the opposite: Sanctification without visible signs: Cornelius the Centurion received the Holy Spirit before baptism (Acts 10:44-48).

Chapter 24: Of the Sacraments

Visible signs without true sanctification:

Simon Magus received baptism but remained in spiritual darkness (Acts 8:13, 18-23).

Therefore, while the sacraments must not be despised or neglected without incurring great impiety and ingratitude toward God, they are not so necessary that salvation is impossible without them. God, who is above His ordinances, can save without them. The danger lies not in the absence of the sacraments but in a willful contempt for them, as Bernard of Clairvaux said.

The Number of Sacraments

There are only two sacraments instituted by Christ in the New Testament: Baptism and the Lord's Supper. No others were ordained by Him. This limited number is a merciful provision for our weakness—few signs for many spiritual truths, yet simple to perform, profound in meaning, and holy in observance.[20]

The five additional sacraments claimed by the Roman Church (penance, matrimony, confirmation, holy orders, and extreme unction) have no warrant in Scripture:

1. Penance and Matrimony: These existed before the New Testament and were necessary under the Old Testament as well.

2. Matrimony: This is not unique to Christianity but is a universal institution, common to all humanity.

---

[20] Augustine, *De Doctrina Christiana*, c. 9.

3. Contradictions: The Roman Church declares that sacraments are necessary for salvation,[21] but forbids priests to marry, even though they claim matrimony is a sacrament. This inconsistency deprives priests of the grace they say marriage confers, undermining their argument for its necessity.

The sacraments, therefore, serve as visible confirmations of God's covenantal promises. They do not impart grace through mechanical performance but are empowered by God's ordinance and the Holy Spirit. Only Baptism and the Lord's Supper stand as true sacraments of the New Testament, given for the edification, assurance, and strengthening of believers in their walk with Christ.

---

[21] Council of Trent, Session 7, Canon 4.

Chapter 25: Of Baptism

Baptism is the sacrament of admission into the Church. By the outward washing or sprinkling of the body with water, the inward cleansing of the soul from sin—through the sprinkling of Christ's blood and the washing of the Holy Spirit—is signed and sealed unto us. The baptism of infants is to be retained in the Church as it aligns with Christ's institution.

Adversaries to this doctrine include:

1. Those who entirely reject baptism, as some ancient heretics and certain modern sects do.

2. Those who permit baptism only for adults but deny it to children, such as the Pelagians and Anabaptists, both holding to the same reasoning.

3. Those who regard baptism as an indifferent matter.

4. Roman Catholics, who declare baptism to be absolutely necessary for salvation, insisting that children who die unbaptized cannot be saved.

5. The same Roman Catholics, who corrupt and adulterate this holy ordinance by adding elements such as salt, spittle, oil, and by performing unnecessary rites including exorcisms and the use of tapers. They even extend baptism to inanimate objects—bells, banners, swords, and daggers—often for violent purposes.

That baptism was ordained and commanded by Christ is explicitly stated in Matthew 28:19, where the promise of salvation is attached (Mark 16:16). Baptism is called the laver of regeneration (Titus 3:5) and "Except a man be born of water and of the Spirit, he cannot enter the kingdom of God," (John 3:5). This does not attribute any part of regeneration to the water itself but demonstrates that the work of the Holy Spirit is symbolized by water—just as fire represents His purifying work (Matthew 3:11). Some misunderstood this and branded their children with hot irons.

Although the outward washing with water does not itself wash away sin, it is referred to as such for the sake of confirming our faith, as the sign is named after what it signifies. Thus, our hearts are persuaded that our sins are as certainly removed by Christ's blood as our bodies are cleansed by water.

Regarding the Roman Catholic additions—such as salt, spittle, and other ceremonies—they are nothing but absurd inventions. The primary controversy today surrounds the timing of baptism. The Pelagians and Anabaptists deny infant baptism, using similar arguments. Unfortunately, many godly individuals have been ensnared by this error despite avoiding the other heresies of the Anabaptist movement.

Their arguments include:

1. There is no explicit precept or example for infant baptism.

Response: There are both precepts and examples that include infants in the Church: Precept: Matthew 28:19 commands baptizing all nations, which includes children as part of those nations. Examples: Acts 16:15, 33 and 1 Corinthians 1:16 mention whole households being baptized, which likely included children. While there may be no explicit command mentioning infants, neither is there any prohibition. Without a stated exception, they must be baptized, or else the general commands and examples are not being fully followed. If the absence of an explicit example invalidates infant baptism, the Anabaptists must stop their own practice of full immersion and "re-baptizing" adults, for there is no explicit command or example for those actions either.

2. Those who do not believe should not be baptized, and infants cannot believe.

Response: This argument misapplies what belongs to adults: The statement "If any would not work, neither should he eat," (2 Thessalonians 3:10), cannot apply to infants because they cannot labor, yet no one denies them nourishment. Infants have reasonable souls capable of understanding and will, which are the faculties of faith. The limitations of their physical development do not hinder the Holy Spirit from working faith in them. If salvation requires faith, and infants cannot have faith, the Anabaptists must provide an alternative way of salvation for infants—or else conclude, cruelly, that all infants who die are damned.

Circumcision was a seal of the righteousness of faith (Romans 4:11) and was administered to infants under the Old Covenant. There is equal reason to baptize infants under the New Covenant. Many examples in Scripture demonstrate children regenerated and sanctified from the womb, such as Jeremiah and John the Baptist. If children can receive the Holy Spirit, they should also receive the sign of baptism. "Can any man forbid water, that these should not be baptized, which have received the Holy Ghost?" (Acts 10:47).

Christ Himself affirmed that children believe in Him (Matthew 18:6), that babes and sucklings praise His name (Matthew 21:16), and that the kingdom of God belongs to such as them. He blessed children, embraced them, and laid His hands upon them, declaring them to be part of God's covenant (Genesis 17:7) and heirs of His promises (Acts 2:39).

The Anabaptists ask how we can know that children believe. Yet do they have an infallible certificate from God confirming the faith of adults? They plunge more unbelievers into their immersion waters than we sprinkle at our fonts.

Their practice of "stripping and dipping" is offensive to modesty and unnecessary. If they insist that there must be an explicit command for every practice, they must concede that they have no such command for full immersion. The Scriptures speak of the "blood of sprinkling," (Hebrews 12:24), and under both the Law and the Gospel, sprinkling signifies purification just as much as immersion.

Chapter 26:
Of the Lord's Supper

The Lord's Supper is the sacrament of preservation in the Church. Through the symbols of bread and wine, the body and blood of Christ are signified, sealed, and offered to every faithful receiver for their spiritual nourishment and continual growth in Him unto everlasting life.

Throughout history, many adversaries have either despised, refused, or profaned this holy sacrament by altering its elements or substituting others in their place. At present, three principal errors persist:

1. **Transubstantiation.** This doctrine holds that, after the words of consecration, the bread and wine are transformed into the actual body and blood of Christ, leaving behind only the appearance of bread and wine to the senses. The substance of the bread and wine supposedly vanishes. The roots of this error trace back to the Capernaites (John 6:52) and were formally established by the Council of Lateran in 1215, against Berengarius. The Roman Church embraces this belief, leading to blasphemous idolatries and elaborate rituals.

2. **Consubstantiation.** This belief attempts to avoid the absurdities of transubstantiation but falls into another error, asserting that the substance of bread and wine coexists with the

physical body and blood of Christ. According to this doctrine, Christ's body is "in, with, and under" the bread. The origins of this view are unclear, though it gained traction with Luther around 1525 and remains held by his followers. This doctrine fueled the practice of bowing and reverencing the communion table as though Christ's physical presence dwelt there.

3. **Bare Symbolism.** This view claims that the sacrament consists solely of bread and wine as mere signs or symbols, with no true presence of Christ beyond their figurative significance. The foundation of this error was laid by heretics roughly four hundred years after Christ, who dismissed the sacrament as having neither benefit nor harm. It resurfaced with Carolostadius around 1524 and is now championed by the Anabaptists.

Our Church adheres to the teaching found in 1 Corinthians 10:16: *"The bread which we break is the communion of the body of Christ."* To refute all three errors:

- If the sacrament contains only bare signs, why does Christ declare, *"This is my body"* and *"This is my blood"*?
- If His body and blood are present in a corporal and carnal manner, why does Christ command, *"Do this in remembrance of me,"* and why does Paul state, *"You proclaim the Lord's death till he come,"* (1 Corinthians 11:26)?

- If Christ is physically present on earth in the sacrament, why does Peter declare that, *"the heavens must receive Him until the time of restitution,"* (Acts 3:21)?

Rejecting both transubstantiation and consubstantiation as exceeding Christ's intent, and rejecting bare symbolism as diminishing it, we affirm a *transmutation*—a profound change in the use of the elements. This change is not in their substance, but in their virtue, power, and spiritual operation. The sanctified signs remain creatures in substance but become mysteries in significance and convey the very realities they symbolize. Christ honors the bread and wine with the titles of His body and blood, not by changing their essence, but by adding grace to their natural use.[22]

In the sacrament, there must be more than mere signs or bare elements. How could earthly bread become an instrument of heavenly grace, capable of quickening and strengthening the soul, without some extraordinary and marvelous change? This change, however, is not in the substance of the elements but in their virtue, power, and spiritual operation. Such efficacy would be impossible unless the body and blood of Christ were truly present, truly given, and truly received in the sacrament. Yet, this presence is not carnal or corporeal—it does not mean

---

[22] Theodoret, *Dialogues*.

that the bread and wine are physically transformed into Christ's flesh and blood, as the Papists claim.

1. This notion contradicts Scripture, for even after consecration, the elements are still referred to as bread and wine (1 Corinthians 11:28).

2. It undermines the nature of a sacrament because a sacrament requires an outward element. Without the element, there can be no sacrament.

3. It defies natural reason, as it suggests that accidents (such as taste, color, or texture) can exist without a substance.

4. Experience confirms that the elements still behave as natural bread and wine—they spoil over time, nourish the body when consumed, and pass through the digestive system. None of this can be said of mere "accidents" or of Christ's glorified body.

5. Even by the Papists' own teaching, mere physical eating without faith is of no benefit. The Council of Trent (Session 13, Chapter 8) and the Roman Catechism both acknowledge this. If faith alone makes the sacrament effectual, why insist upon a physical transformation?

6. Their argument is inconsistent even with their canon law, which cites Augustine: "To what purpose would the Lord commend a mystery if the substance of the sacrament were already fully realized?"

Objection: But Christ plainly said, "This is my body"—and at a solemn moment, the night before His death. This was no time for obscure parables but for clear and plain words.

Response: Christ also said, "This is my blood," while holding the cup (Mark 14:23-24). If taken literally, the cup itself—and not merely the wine—must have been transformed into blood. Yet even their most subtle theologians admit that the phrase concerning the cup is figurative. If one phrase is figurative, why not the other?

When Christ said, "This is my body," He was not declaring the nature of the bread but the nature of His body—that His body is spiritual nourishment for the soul, just as bread is nourishment for the body. This phrase does not indicate a transformation of one substance into another but illustrates the relationship between the two. The same Jesus who earlier called Himself the "bread of life" in John 6 now calls the bread His body, using a change of terms to illustrate the change brought about by grace. The purpose is not to focus on what we see with our eyes but to direct our hearts toward the unseen realities of faith. Theodoret remarked in his dialogues: "Why do you prepare your teeth and your stomach? This is not food for the body but for the soul. Believe, and you have eaten."[23]

Consubstantiation, the belief that Christ's body is present "in, with, and under" the bread, strays even further from the truth than transubstantiation. Christ

---

[23] Augustine, *Tractate* 25 on John 6.

did not say, "My body is in the bread" but simply, "This is my body." Both errors lead to idolatry and are far removed from the original meaning of Christ's words, the teachings of the apostles (1 Corinthians 11), and the testimony of the early Church Fathers, who referred to the elements as signs, figures, and types of Christ's body and blood. Augustine himself declared that the phrase "This is my body" must be understood figuratively, not literally.[24] Moreover, both doctrines propose ideas that are impossible according to natural reason.

But setting aside the barren opinion of a mere sign or figure, the true question between us and others is not about the substance of what is received—we readily confess that the very body and blood of Christ is given and received. The real dispute lies in the *manner* of this reception. They claim that it is received corporally and carnally; we affirm that it is indeed received truly and really—if by really one means truly and indeed—but that this reception is spiritual, heavenly, and divine.

The Apostle makes clear the reality of the thing itself in 1 Corinthians 10:16, "The bread which we break, is it not the communion of the body of Christ?" Yet, for the manner of this presence, we are not given the same degree of explicit explanation.

To conclude, the truth of Christ's body and blood is present with the signs; the Holy Spirit accompanies the sacrament, feeding our souls with the

---

[24] Augustine, Book 3, On Christian Doctrine.

reality of Christ's sacrifice. However, the inward, invisible working of the Divine Spirit in this mystery is beyond human comprehension—the natural man cannot grasp it because it is spiritual in nature.

Let us, therefore, believe firmly what we cannot fully conceive. We can rest assured that in the Lord's Supper, we truly receive the body and blood of Christ by faith, even though our senses and reason cannot fathom the depth of this divine mystery.

Chapter 27: Of Reformation

There is no particular Church on earth—nor has there ever been—so privileged as to be free from the possibility of falling into serious errors in both life and doctrine. History bears witness that no Church composed of human beings is immune to error and, therefore, all may require reformation, just as a material building periodically needs repair.

Because many grievous abuses and superstitions were recently introduced into the Church of England—through the deceitfulness of some—to the dishonor of Almighty God, the decline of piety, and the imminent ruin of true Protestant faith, the necessity for this present reformation became urgent. This reformation, however, is not an innovation but rather a restoration of our Church to its original purity in doctrine, discipline, and divine worship, as established by the noble rulers King Edward VI and Queen Elizabeth of renowned memory.

Though this truth is as evident as daylight—demonstrable upon examination—and though the current reformation has purged many flagrant errors that were contrary to the Church's determinations, there remain numerous adversaries who, out of malice, ignorance, or both, oppose it with all their strength.

These opponents can be grouped into three categories:

Chapter 27: Of Reformation

1. Malicious Opponents: These include dissolute and lawless individuals who abhor any reformation that curbs their sinful lifestyles and restrains their ungodly habits. Among them are certain Papists and sectarians.

2. Ignorant Opponents: These are civil Protestants who mistakenly assume that no religion could be older or truer than the one in which *they were raised*. Confusing the officeholders of the Church with the Church itself, they adopt their religious views based solely on the credibility of their leaders.

3. Malicious and Ignorant Opponents: These are fiery zealots who believe the only way to reform the Church is to dismantle it entirely, as if the only remedy for a headache were to destroy the head itself. Additionally, there are hypocrites who push for reformation only to serve their selfish ambitions, yet secretly oppose its truth as fiercely as any of the aforementioned adversaries.

I aim to address the sincere Protestant who opposes the reformation out of misguidance, hoping they will embrace the truth once freed from the falsehoods spread by the many deceivers in the world.

A common lament is heard: "Bring back the religion of Queen Elizabeth's time! We no longer have the same religion!"

To this, the brief response is: We do still have the same religion—it has not changed but has been preserved. What we possess today is the true Protestant religion once professed, now not altered but purified—

restored to its original state and cleansed from the corruptions that had recently invaded it.

For example, during recent years: Numerous Popish and Arminian doctrines were publicly taught and defended—doctrines at odds with the Church's foundational teachings. A comparison with the *Thirty-Nine Articles*, the *Book of Homilies*, the *Nine Articles of Lambeth*, and the works of our former bishops makes this evident.

Secondly, many crucifixes, images, or idols were set up in our most prominent churches and their most conspicuous places—partly by connivance and partly by the direct command of men who then held prominent authority. This fostered superstition and led to acts of idolatry. However, such images are contrary:

1. To the Word of God, which expressly forbids them.

2. To the judgment of the early Christians, as well as the Fathers and Councils, who condemned such practices with great zeal.

3. To the stance of the Church of England itself, as made evident in the Book of Homilies and the Thirty-Nine Articles.

Thirdly, the Communion Table was altered in both name and placement—changed from a table to an altar, and moved from the body of the church to the upper end of the chancel. This change opposed the explicit instructions in the Book of Common Prayer, which states that the table should stand "in the body of the church or in the chancel" and that "the priest shall stand at the north side." The priest cannot stand at the north side if the table is pressed against the wall. Even if some discretion is allowed to the ordinary regarding placement, it requires more than ordinary discretion to redefine the end of a table as its side—an attempt once made, though the geometry failed.

Fourthly, the practice of *bowing* to the Communion Table was of graver consequence than many realized. This act is a remnant of the errors of Transubstantiation and Consubstantiation, reinforcing these heresies in people's minds. It introduces further popish superstitions and fosters the potential for gross idolatry.

Fifthly, the use of rails, wainscots, and curtains before the Communion Table—making it resemble the Holy of Holies of the Jews or a chapel prepared for private Mass—suggested that none but the priest was holy enough to approach. Additional ceremonies, such as the use of tapers, copes, vestments, and other paraphernalia, although dismissed by some as minor matters, were not harmless due to their size. Like small thieves creeping through the windows to unlock doors for larger ones, these practices would have eventually reintroduced the entire mass of Popish idolatry. Those who defend such practices serve as Satan's accomplices, seducing the people and leading them into idolatry under the guise of "indifferent things."

Additionally, there was a grievous misuse of excommunication, the Church's highest form of censure. In the ecclesiastical courts, it became a tool for collecting fees, with individuals being cast out of the Church for failing to appear in court—a reprehensible perversion of discipline.

Finally, it is equally condemnable to scornfully or irreverently abuse the Church and places set apart for God's ordinances. Such behavior often reflects contempt for the ordinances themselves. A cautionary example is that of Julian, the uncle of the apostate emperor, who in contempt urinated against the Communion Table. He was struck down by divine judgment, his bowels rotting, and he ultimately vomited his own excrement. Our own times have not been without similar examples of impiety met with God's justice.

Despite this, while we acknowledge that God hears us in all places when we call upon Him, it is fitting and proper that places designated for holy worship be set apart and adorned with appropriate and reverent decor befitting their sacred purpose.

There remains one significant issue that causes many to stumble—the strict examination of communicants and the suspension of some individuals from the Lord's Supper for certain reasons. To remove this misunderstanding, it must be noted that this practice is simply the minister's duty as prescribed by the Orders of our own Church, as outlined in the Book

Chapter 27: Of Reformation

of Common Prayer. Therefore, it is not an innovation but a continuation of established practice.

Considering these points, we can see the error of many who, *under the guise* of defending Protestantism, oppose the very reforms meant to preserve it. They believe they can uphold the Church of England while using methods that will, in reality, destroy it. Let all true-hearted Protestants reflect on these matters and, out of love for the Church of England, defend her against those who have so grievously abused her. These deceitful actors, under the pretense of authority, have sold the people counterfeit doctrines that the Church of England has always condemned, not commended.

If there has been any change in our Church beyond what has been mentioned, it concerns circumstances, not substance. The body remains the same—only its attire has changed. As one eminent doctor in our Church (no friend to novelty) once said, clerical habits and vestments are not the essence of religion but its outward wrappings, much like swaddling clothes. There is a time to lay such things aside. All ceremonies were regarded as changeable by those who first instituted them. As the philosopher said of his son, "I knew I begot a mortal being," so they understood that their decrees were not unalterable laws of the Medes and Persians. They expected future generations to change these rites when good reason called for it, just as they had abolished many earlier practices. This perspective is evident in the prefaces to the *Book of Common Prayer*.

Some argue that the removal of bishops is a stain on the Reformation. But let me ask: did grand palaces, vast retinues, and lofty titles align with the poverty, meekness, and humility of Christ, whom they claimed to serve? Here is a simple test of the legitimacy of such things: let a prayer be composed specifically petitioning Almighty God to restore bishops' wealth, titles, and estates by name. Who would dare approach God with such a request on their lips? We can pray for things that are lawful and morally sound with confidence—but if a person cannot sincerely pray for something, their conscience has already judged it as unlawful.

Finally, some lament that the Church has been trodden down, its lands and goods taken. But when they speak of the Church, they often mean the lands held by the bishops. If these lands are taken from the bishops and restored to their rightful purposes—ensuring that every church has its proper means of support and that those who labor for the Gospel receive due provision—is that sacrilege, or is it justice? When the bishops held multiple tithes and revenues that rightly belonged to other ministers who faithfully served their congregations, was that not a form of sacrilege? Resources that are not owed to others can, and should, be used to establish a more effective ministry, meeting the urgent needs of the Church in all places.

Chapter 28: Of Toleration

Although the heathens had countless gods and as many different religions, ceremonies, and forms of worship, we never read of any disputes among them regarding religious differences. The reason for this was that the so-called gods of the heavens, as someone once said, were "good fellows," content to share among themselves the glory that was not rightly theirs. In contrast, the true God is a jealous God who will not share His glory with another, as it belongs solely to Him.

This fundamental truth reveals why the demand for toleration of all religions is a strong argument against the sectaries. Their desire for such toleration demonstrates that they are not of God, for God cannot permit the acceptance of falsehood alongside His truth. John's Gospel warns that even a small error must be addressed and corrected. This teaches us never to tolerate even the smallest deviation from truth, for tolerating "tares" allows them to grow until they threaten to choke out the "wheat."

We must follow the example of Paul in Galatians 1:5, who would not yield to false brethren for even an hour, so that the truth of the Gospel might be preserved. In the same way, we must not yield to error, no matter how insignificant it may seem. As Paul wrote to Titus (Titus 1:11), false teachers' mouths "must be stopped" because their words spread like a deadly infection (2 Timothy 2:17). Though false doctrines may appear small at first, they can grow until they consume the very heart and soul of true religion. Therefore, toleration of false religion is not an act of kindness but a gateway to spiritual ruin.

FINIS.

A Gainful Death: The End of a Truly Christian Life

A Sermon at the Funeral of Mr. John Griffith, Late Minister of the Gospel, Who Departed This Life on May 16th, in the 79th Year of His Age.
Preached May 20th, 1700.

Philippians 1:21, "For to me to live is Christ, and to die is gain."

As I was somewhat surprised when asked to preach this funeral sermon, I do not doubt that some here may also wonder why I undertook this task. Let me assure you that it was solely the earnest appeals of his beloved friends and relations, together with my own profound respect for the deceased, that persuaded me to comply.

Having agreed, I considered carefully which Scripture should serve as the foundation for this solemn discourse. After much thought, I concluded that no words could be more appropriate than these excellent words of the Apostle Paul. I chose them because they brought immense comfort to the reverend minister whose life we commemorate today. These very words sustained and encouraged him in his final days and were spoken by him with great joy just hours before his passing.

This text, therefore, provides the most fitting meditation for this occasion, especially since they were spoken by someone not unlike our departed friend—though differing in degree—the Apostle Paul, a faithful servant of Christ. Like our friend, Paul was an aged minister of the Gospel. At the time he penned these words, he was imprisoned in Rome and expecting an imminent death—not due to old age or illness as with our departed brother, but as a martyr for Christ. Yet, despite the looming shadow of death, Paul's heart was full of peace and joy, as evidenced in verse 20 of this chapter.

The source of this holy confidence and his fearless anticipation of death was his certainty that Christ was his life. Therefore, he viewed death not as loss, but as gain, as declared in the text: "For to me to live is Christ, and to die is gain."

In this verse, we see two main points:

1. The Apostle's description of the Christian life: "For to me to live is Christ."

2. The blessed death of a Christian: "To die is gain."

Let us consider the first point. Some translations, such as that of Tremellius from the Syriac, render this phrase as "Christ is my life," showing that the infinitive "to live" is used in place of the noun "life." This usage is common both in Scripture and in other writings. Interpreted this way, the phrase teaches us that Christ is the life of a true Christian, as also stated in Colossians

3:4, "When Christ, who is our life, shall appear, then shall ye also appear with him in glory."

The second point concerns the blessed death of those for whom Christ is their life. Those who can truly say, with the Apostle, that Christ is their life, can also be assured that death will be gain, not terror.

Doctrine: *All those—and only those—who have Christ as their life will find death to be gain.*

In explaining this truth, I will address two main points:

1. What is included in Christ being the life of a true Christian.

2. The advantages gained by such a one in death.

What is Included in Christ's Being the Life of a True Christian. To understand what it means for Christ to be the life of a true Christian, we must examine the details of this phrase. By doing so, we can reflect on our own spiritual condition. Here are the key points that I believe are included:

1. Christ as the Meritorious Cause of a Christian's Life. We are all, because of sin, spiritually dead under the law and subject to condemnation. However, a true Christian is brought from this state of death and condemnation into a state of justification and life. How does this happen? It is by being "justified freely by his grace through the redemption that is in Christ Jesus," (Romans 3:24). Through the meritorious sufferings and obedience of Christ, believers receive the saving benefits of His work. By sin, all humanity has

become estranged from the life of God, but a true Christian is raised from spiritual death to a life of sincere holiness by the gracious operation of the Holy Spirit, "which he shed on us abundantly through Jesus Christ our Saviour," (Titus 3:6).

2. Christ as the Principle of Spiritual Life. The spiritual life of a true Christian flows from union with Christ. It is a dangerous error to believe that one can live a life of justification without also experiencing a life of sanctification. Yet sanctification is impossible without vital union with Christ. The Apostle Paul declares, "I live; yet not I, but Christ liveth in me: and the life which I now live in the flesh I live by the faith of the Son of God, who loved me, and gave himself for me," (Galatians 2:20).

3. Christ's Laws as the Governing Rule of the Christian's Life. If we truly receive Christ, we receive Him as Lord. "As ye have therefore received Christ Jesus the Lord, so walk ye in him," (Colossians 2:6). We must willingly accept Him as our King to rule and govern us, saving us not only from the penalty of sin but also from its present power and dominion. We receive Him as our great High Priest, who atones for our guilt and maintains our peace with God through His sacrifice and intercession. "He became the author of eternal salvation unto all them that obey him," (Hebrews 5:9).

4. The Love of Christ as the Driving Motive. The love of Christ compels and constrains the true Christian. Only those who can declare, "The love of Christ

constraineth us," (2 Corinthians 5:14), can also, with confidence, say that death is gain. The "crown of righteousness" is promised "to all them that love his appearing," (2 Timothy 4:8). None can love His appearing unless they first say, "We love him, because he first loved us," (1 John 4:19).

5. Christ as the Pattern and Example of the Christian's Life. God has predestined all His children to be conformed to the image of His Son, "that he might be the firstborn among many brethren," (Romans 8:29). This conformity involves grace and holiness in this life and glory and happiness in the life to come. The former is the necessary path to the latter. It is in vain to claim salvation in Christ without striving to reflect His character—His holiness, humility, meekness, self-denial, and zeal for the glory of God. "He that saith he abideth in him ought himself also so to walk, even as he walked," (1 John 2:6).

6. The Glory and Honor of Christ as the End of the Christian's Life. A true Christian does not merely speak or act for Christ on occasion; their whole life is lived for Him. Paul rejoiced when Christ was preached and glorified, even though the preachers sometimes did so out of envy and sought to undermine him. What mattered most to Paul was that Christ's name was exalted. In this, we must follow Paul's example, proving that Christ is truly our life. Only then can we, with the same confidence, declare that death will be gain.

These six points describe the meaning behind the phrase "To me to live is Christ." When taken together, they present a full description of a true, living Christian. A Christian is one who, through Christ's sufferings and obedience, is vitally united to Him by faith, justified, sanctified, ruled by His laws, compelled by His love, conformed to His life, and devoted to His glory and honor.

II. The Advantage Gained by Death. Having understood what it means for Christ to be the life of a Christian, we can now consider the gain that comes through death. This can be understood both generally and particularly.

1. Death as an Immediate Gain. For every true Christian, death is not merely an eventual gain—it is an immediate one. When the body returns to the earth, "the spirit shall return unto God who gave it," (Ecclesiastes 12:7). This is why heavenly-minded Christians long to be "absent from the body, and to be present with the Lord," (2 Corinthians 5:8). If this were not the case, how could Paul declare, "Having a desire to depart, and to be with Christ; which is far better," (Philippians 1:23)?

Our Savior also affirms this truth in His promise to the penitent thief on the cross: "Verily I say unto thee, To day shalt thou be with me in paradise," (Luke 23:43). This clearly teaches that upon death, the souls of the faithful are immediately received into heavenly bliss. Christ demonstrated this Himself when He commended

His spirit to His Father, saying, "Father, into thy hands I commend my spirit," (Luke 23:46).

2. The Fulfillment and Completion of Gain at Christ's Glorious Appearing. The fullness and perfection of the gain that Christians receive through death will be realized at the glorious appearance of the Lord Jesus Christ. When the bodies of the saints are raised and reunited with their souls, they will fully enter into the joy of their Lord. This future event is often described in Scripture as the "great day of redemption" and "the day of recompense." It is "when Christ, who is our life, shall appear" that believers "shall also appear with him in glory," (Colossians 3:4). At that time, Christ will "come to be glorified in his saints, and to be admired in all them that believe," (2 Thessalonians 1:10). Those who have fought the good fight and kept the faith will enter into their final reward, anticipating the "crown of righteousness," (2 Timothy 4:8), which will be given at His appearing.

Having considered this general truth, let us now examine more specifically the advantages that Christians gain through death.

1. Freedom from All Sin. The first great gain of death for the Christian is perfect freedom from sin. For any serious believer, this is undoubtedly a tremendous gain. While believers are described as being "made free from sin," (Romans 6:18), this freedom refers only to the dominion of sin and not to its complete eradication. The Apostle Paul explains this when he speaks of being

"made free from the law of sin and death," (Romans 8:2). Absolute and perfect freedom from sin is reserved for the life to come.

In this life, remnants of sin still cling to the believer, like a deep-seated leprosy that cannot be fully cured without the dissolution of the earthly house of the body. Death is, the means by which Christ completes His work, presenting His Church "glorious, not having spot, or wrinkle, or any such thing, but...holy and without blemish," (Ephesians 5:27). At last, believers will stand "without fault before the throne of God," (Revelation 14:5).

2. Freedom from Temptation and the Inclination to Sin. Death not only frees believers from sin itself but also from every temptation and inclination to sin. This freedom surpasses the first in its magnitude. Our first parents, though sinless in their original state of innocence, were still susceptible to temptation—and tragically fell. Even our Lord Jesus Christ, though "holy, harmless, undefiled," (Hebrews 7:26), was subjected to severe temptations during His earthly life. The devil assaulted Him with the most vile and hellish temptations. Although He was never for a moment inclined to sin, He still "suffered, being tempted," (Hebrews 2:18). This suffering implies the real burden and agony of resisting temptation.

If Christ Himself endured such trials, how much more do His followers, who often feel the sharpness of temptation and the weakness of their flesh? Although grace may preserve them from falling, the struggle is real, and many live in fear of yielding. Yet death liberates the Christian not only from the destructive power of Satan's fiery darts but also from their troubling presence. Believers will be freed from "fleshly lusts, which war against the soul," (1 Peter 2:11), and from the world's corrupt influences. Death delivers them entirely from this present evil world (Galatians 1:4).

In this respect, death ushers the believer into a far more excellent life than even the life of grace experienced here on earth. Though believers may feel secure in their spiritual standing, they are always warned to "take heed lest they fall," (1 Corinthians 10:12). Even the most mature Christian must, like the Apostle Paul, maintain vigilance, "lest...I myself should be a castaway," (1 Corinthians 9:27).

Death places the believer in a state far surpassing the original paradise of Adam and Eve. Though our first parents were free from sin and possessed the ability to remain in that state, they were not free from the possibility of falling, as their tragic story reveals. In contrast, death secures the Christian in a state of holiness that is both impeccable and immutable.

3. Freedom from Sorrow and Misery. Finally, death frees the living Christian from all sorrow and misery. In this life, believers are already exempt from future wrath and condemnation due to their justification through Christ. However, the sorrows of this earthly life—the trials, pains, and

disappointments—continue to afflict them until death. Upon death, they will enter a state where "God shall wipe away all tears from their eyes; and there shall be no more death, neither sorrow, nor crying, neither shall there be any more pain," (Revelation 21:4). The burdens of sickness, grief, persecution, and loss will be forever removed.

In death, the Christian finds perfect rest and relief. As Jesus said, "Come unto me, all ye that labour and are heavy laden, and I will give you rest," (Matthew 11:28). This rest is fully realized when the soul departs to be with Christ. Free from all sin, temptation, and suffering, the believer enters into the eternal joy of the Lord, where every affliction is exchanged for everlasting comfort and glory.

God Hath Not Appointed His Children to Wrath

God has not destined His people to suffer wrath but rather to obtain salvation through Jesus Christ (1 Thessalonians 5:9). Yet, as long as sin remains in their nature, they must endure sorrows and afflictions, which are inseparable companions of sin. Job's lament is as true for the most devout Christians as for all humanity: "Man that is born of a woman is of few days, and full of trouble," (Job 14:1).

How many sorrows afflict some through poverty and need, while others find no less grief in acquiring and managing riches. And how often even greater anguish overtakes them when, through some unforeseen calamity, they suffer the sudden loss of wealth as their "riches make themselves wings, and fly away as an eagle toward heaven," (Proverbs 23:5).

Many times, believers are troubled by the hostility of open enemies; at other times, they are equally pained by the treachery of false friends or the disloyalty of those who were once genuine companions. The children of God frequently bear bodily pains and grievous afflictions, enduring illnesses and distempers. At the same time, they may also suffer spiritual sorrows due to doubts and fears that besiege their minds.

There are heartbreaking sorrows caused by the sinful actions of children or other close relations. At times, they must also endure the piercing grief of losing a loved one suddenly to death's cruel stroke. The list of sorrows that afflict God's people is almost endless. But, at the moment of their departure, God will "wipe away all tears from their eyes; and there shall be no more death, neither sorrow, nor crying, neither shall there be any more pain: for the former things are passed away," (Revelation 21:4).

Freedom from the Burden of a Sinful and Animal Body

Death not only frees the Christian from the burden of sin but also from the limitations of the natural body. A sinful body and an animal body are distinct. It would be blasphemous and false to say that our Lord Jesus had a sinful body. However, it is true that He possessed a natural body like ours—subject to the same physical weaknesses and infirmities, though not the moral corruption that sin has wrought in our bodies.

In this way, He is described as being sent "in the likeness of sinful flesh," (Romans 8:3), not as one with sinful flesh itself. The bodies of saints, even in their redeemed state, remain a source of much weakness. Though they may no longer lead believers into sin, they remain a hindrance—like a dead weight that holds the aspiring soul back from ascending to greater heights in contemplation and communion with God.

Even though the flesh may no longer reign over the believer, it still proves to be a sluggish and resistant servant. The spirit may be willing, but the flesh remains weak (Matthew 26:41), often impeding the Christian in their devotions and duties. This is why the saints must continually watch and pray for divine assistance, lest they fall prey to temptation.

The Glorious Transformation of the Body

But death will bring the Christian into a state where this frail and corruptible body is transformed into something glorious. The once weak and perishable body will be raised in power; the earthly body will become heavenly and immortal. Paul describes this transformation beautifully, "It is sown in dishonor; it is raised in glory: it is sown in weakness; it is raised in power, it is sown a natural body; it is raised a spiritual body," (1 Corinthians 15:43-44).

In that state, believers will not merely symbolically, but literally, rise with renewed strength—

"they shall mount up with wings as eagles; they shall run, and not be weary; and they shall walk, and not faint," (Isaiah 40:31).

In short, our Redeemer will "change our vile body, that it may be fashioned like unto his glorious body" (Philippians 3:21), using the same mighty power by which He is able to subdue all things to Himself. What a glorious hope and a gainful promise this is for every living Christian at the moment of death.

The souls of believers, at and after death, are freed not only from sin but also from the affliction of ignorance and made perfect in the knowledge of God and His excellent works. Our Savior calls this knowledge "life eternal" (John 17:3), for as a sanctified knowledge of God leads to eternal life, the perfection of that knowledge constitutes the very essence of eternal blessedness.

Even the most enlightened saints must, like Elihu, acknowledge that they cannot order their thoughts and words rightly concerning God due to the darkness of their understanding (Job 37:19). The highest notions and most profound discourses of an apostle regarding the mysteries of God are but as the broken speech of children compared to the knowledge they shall possess in heaven. From this deficiency arise differing opinions even among sincere Christians, leading to disputes over matters that neither fully comprehends.

But death will strip away the scales from their eyes and remove the veils from their hearts. Their current dim and partial knowledge will disappear like the faint flicker of a candle before the brilliance of the sun. The Apostle Paul speaks to this transformation, "For now we see through a glass, darkly; but then face to face: now I know in part; but then shall I know even as also I am known," (1 Corinthians 13:12).

Then, the saints will behold the mysteries of redemption—those wonders that the angels themselves long to understand (1 Peter 1:12). The intricate workings of divine providence, which now seem so perplexing, will be revealed in their full beauty and wisdom. As the book of Ecclesiastes says, "Better is the end of a thing than the beginning thereof," (Ecclesiastes 7:8). When the saints see God's providence from the beginning to the end, they will finally perceive the depths of His wisdom and goodness in all His works, and they will gaze in wonder and delight at His glorious plans.

Death will also bring believers into the beatific vision—the immediate and full enjoyment of God and their blessed Redeemer. The pure in heart will see God, as promised by our Savior (Matthew 5:8). "They shall see his face; and his name shall be in their foreheads," (Revelation 22:4). How this vision will occur, no human mind can fully conceive, nor can any pen or tongue adequately describe it. But we have this assurance from

Scripture, "We shall see him as he is; and we shall be like him," (1 John 3:2). This vision will transform and glorify the saints, conforming them to His likeness.

It is unchristian to murmur at the death of godly friends and relatives, for their passing is but the fulfillment of Christ's mediatorial request, "Father, I will that they also, whom thou hast given me, be with me where I am; that they may behold my glory," (John 17:24). What greater joy could there be than to dwell forever in the presence of the Lord? For those who count it both a duty and a privilege to seek His glory now, even through the glass of ordinances, the thought of beholding Him face to face is the utmost desire of their hearts. The psalmist's cry is theirs: "My soul thirsteth for God, for the living God: when shall I come and appear before God?" (Psalm 42:2). And again: "My soul thirsteth for thee, to see thy power and thy glory, so as I have seen thee in the sanctuary," (Psalm 63:2).

Death also ushers the saint into the most blessed and delightful society. Even now, Christians enjoy fellowship with one another and an invisible communion with angels, who minister to them as heirs of salvation (Hebrews 1:14). But in heaven, they will ascend from the valley of death to the heights of Mount Zion, "the city of the living God, the heavenly Jerusalem, and to an innumerable company of angels, to the general assembly and church of the firstborn, which are written in heaven, and to God the Judge of all, and to the spirits of just men made perfect," (Hebrews 12:22-23).

The saints in heaven are made perfect—freed from all the imperfections and flaws in knowledge and holiness that sometimes make even the fellowship of believers on earth difficult. What joy it will be to meet again with dear friends and family, now perfected in Christ! And perhaps, by God's grace, to meet even those who were once estranged or counted as enemies, now fully reconciled.

What unspeakable happiness it will be to commune with Abraham, Isaac, Jacob, the patriarchs, prophets, apostles, and martyrs—indeed, with all the noble saints whose lives of faith we have admired and whose names we have read. How great a privilege to join their number and dwell with them forever in perfect harmony, rejoicing in the presence of our Lord and King. Death will bring the believer into the most profound and untainted joys. In this life, even the most refined pleasures are mingled with sorrow. The greatest delights are often accompanied by pain, anxiety, or unease. Worldly prosperity is often achieved through care, maintained with fear, and lost in grief. Honor and power often bring discomfort to those who possess them and envy to those who do not. Knowledge, which is among the sweetest pursuits of an enlightened mind, can bring its own burden. As the wisest of men once declared, "For in much wisdom is much grief: and he that increaseth knowledge increaseth sorrow," (Ecclesiastes 1:18). Even the spiritual joys of religion are often dampened—whether by a sense of our imperfections, by melancholy of spirit, or by the enemy of souls, who seeks to darken our path to heaven if he cannot drag us to hell.

But death ushers the souls of the righteous into the immediate presence of God, "where there is fulness of joy; at his right hand there are pleasures for evermore," (Psalm 16:11). The doubts that once burdened sincere souls will be exchanged for perfect assurance. Their mourning will turn to melodies, their sighs to songs of praise, and their sorrows to joyful hallelujahs to Him who sits on the throne and to the Lamb forever and ever (Revelation 5:13).

The eternal nature of these joys must also be noted. While eternity may seem a mere circumstance, it is *essential* to the perfection of heavenly bliss. Imagine the anguish if a saint, amid the heights of heavenly delight, were to fear its eventual loss. The very thought would cast a shadow over even the brightest joy. But this can never happen. As Job lamented the fleeting miseries of life, "I would not live alway," (Job 7:16), no such thought will ever enter the mind of a glorified saint. Knowing that joy will last forever is an integral part of their bliss. The Apostle Paul spoke of the believer's reward as a "weight of glory"—not only for its greatness but also for its permanence (2 Corinthians 4:17).

Consider, then, how *blessed* it is to be born again. Those who are regenerated have an inheritance that is "incorruptible, and undefiled, and that fadeth not away, reserved in heaven," (1 Peter 1:4-5). This inheritance is not like the perishable inheritances of this world. It is secure, guarded by the power of God through faith for salvation.

Having explored the manifold advantages believers gain through death, I cannot help but affirm that even the most eloquent words only begin to describe this gain. Whoever passes through the dark valley of death into those regions of light and blessedness will surely exclaim, as the Queen of Sheba did of Solomon's wisdom, "Behold, the half was not told me," (1 Kings 10:7). The glory and felicity of that state far exceed anything they had imagined.

Let me now offer some reflections on this great truth.

First, we may infer the wisdom of sincere religion. If this is the end of a Christian life, then surely true religion and piety are the highest wisdom. Reason itself must agree that it is wiser to prefer the living fountain over broken cisterns that hold no water, to value our souls over our bodies, heaven over earth, eternity over time, and lasting joys over fleeting pleasures. Therefore, the genuinely religious person is indeed the truly wise one.

Second, we see the folly of neglecting the life that leads to this gainful death. How astonishingly foolish it is to disregard Christ, who alone can give us life! What madness it is to neglect the salvation He offers! Equally foolish is it to cling to an empty form of godliness without its power, thinking that mere outward observance will suffice while indulging in secret sin. Such individuals have no part in this blessed hope.

Hypocrites may now lull themselves into a false sense of security, boasting in their profession and privileges while remaining indifferent to the holiness required of true believers. But their hope will perish, and their trust will prove as fragile as a spider's web (Job 8:14). Though they may flatter themselves and suppress the truth with lies, they will one day be awakened from their delusions. When they stand before the all-knowing Judge, their empty claims will be exposed, and He will declare with terrifying finality, "I never knew you: depart from me, ye that work iniquity," (Matthew 7:23).

For such souls, death will not be gain—it will be the end of all their fleeting delights and the beginning of everlasting sorrow and woe.

Seeing that none will be admitted into heaven but those who have Christ as their life, we should, as much as lies within our power, admit and retain only such persons in Christ's Church. The Church is intended to be an emblem of heaven and is often called the Kingdom of Heaven for this reason. Those who make Christ's laws the rule of their lives, Christ's life the pattern for their own, and His glory and interest their ultimate end and design—these alone bring honor to the Church and truly benefit from its fellowship. A single scandalous sinner allowed to remain in the Church can corrupt the whole body, for, as the Scripture teaches, "a little leaven leaveneth the whole lump," (1 Corinthians 5:6). The entire Church becomes guilty by condoning such sin.

It is a grievous reproach to our holy religion to allow such individuals to remain in Christian fellowship, especially if that person holds a place of honor as a teacher. Many of the Greek Fathers have pointed out that the incestuous fornicator in Corinth (1 Corinthians 5:1-2) was likely esteemed for his eloquence and learning, which caused the Corinthians to be puffed up rather than humbled. Instead of mourning his sin, they gloried in their tolerance of his wickedness. To this, the Apostle warns: "Look diligently lest any root of bitterness springing up trouble you, and thereby many be defiled. Lest there be any fornicator or profane person," (Hebrews 12:15-16).

This should also persuade all who have Christ as their life to love one another. All such believers are born from above and are therefore strangers and pilgrims here on earth. Their time on earth is but a brief sojourning, "For here have we no continuing city, but we seek one to come," (Hebrews 13:14). Though they live in the world, they are not of it. They are God's elect, His peculiar treasure, chosen by their Redeemer out of the world, "Therefore the world hateth them," (John 15:19). Just as they are alienated from the world in their hearts and actions, so they are no longer strangers and foreigners to heaven but fellow citizens with the saints and members of God's household, (Ephesians 2:19).

Consider how travelers from the same country, even if they were strangers to each other at home, become closely united when they meet in a foreign and hostile land, especially when they share common hardships. How much more, then, should Christians, who are fellow travelers through the wilderness of this world toward the celestial Canaan, heed the counsel that good Joseph gave his brothers, "See that ye fall not out by the way," (Genesis 45:24).

If Christ is our life, we are members of one body, partakers of one Spirit, and called in the same hope of our calling. We are subjects and disciples of one Lord, hold to one saving faith, and are children of the same God and Father (Ephesians 4:4-6). These are powerful reasons for unity and love. If, in addition to all this, we have been visibly initiated into Christ's Church by the one baptism He ordained, then differing opinions on minor matters of religion should never hinder us from striving together to keep "the unity of the Spirit in the bond of peace," (Ephesians 4:3).

This truth offers immense comfort when our godly friends and family are taken from us by death. While we may have reason to mourn their absence, we should not grieve as those who have no hope (1 Thessalonians 4:13). They have only fallen asleep in Jesus and will surely awaken to be with the Lord forever.

To you, the family of our departed brother, you have cause to mourn your loss, and the Church of Christ mourns hers. But you also have much reason for comfort, as God blessed you with his presence for many years. His long life of faith, crowned with righteousness, is evidence of God's favor: "The hoary head is a crown of glory, if it be found in the way of righteousness," (Proverbs 16:31). He lived nearly eighty years, over sixty of which were devoted to the service of the Lord. For fifty-four years, he labored as a pastor and overseer under the Great Shepherd and Bishop of souls. Fourteen of those years were spent in suffering, bonds, and imprisonment for the sake of Christ and in defense of a good conscience.

In some respects, he may have been considered too strict in his views regarding Church communion. Yet this, too, seems to have stemmed from his sincere zeal and deep reverence for the laws of Christ. In his long profession of faith, I know of no dishonor or blemish he brought upon our holy religion. Rather, he was an ornament and testimony to it.

He endured his prolonged illness and pain with *remarkable* patience and submission to God's will. To the very end, he rejoiced, in the full assurance of his hope. Knowing that Christ was his life, he confidently concluded that death would be his gain. We have good reason to believe, through God's grace, that he is now among those blessed ones who "die in the Lord," rest from their labors, and whose works follow them (Revelation 14:13). He will undoubtedly hear that joyful declaration, "Well done, thou good and faithful servant... enter thou into the joy of thy Lord," (Matthew 25:21).

Sermon: A Gainful Death

Let us leave him there, in his heavenly rest, and consider our own ways.

In this final exhortation, I urge you to follow his example, as far as he followed Christ (1 Corinthians 11:1), and to imitate all those who, through faith and patience, inherit the promises (Hebrews 6:12). Be diligent in your pursuit of grace and holiness so that you may make your calling and election sure (2 Peter 1:10) and receive an abundant entrance into the everlasting kingdom of our Lord and Savior Jesus Christ (2 Peter 1:11).

This faithful minister lived a full life, but who among us can guarantee such a long span? "What is your life? It is even a vapor, that appeareth for a little time, and then vanisheth away," (James 4:14). Remember that even the youngest, the strongest, and the healthiest among us live but a fleeting life and walk in vanity (Psalm 39:5-6). Therefore, we must earnestly pray and seek wisdom from above, numbering our days aright, that we may apply our hearts to true wisdom (Psalm 90:12).

We have seen our friends and loved ones suddenly cut down like flowers, unexpectedly taken from us. Let us thank God for the hope we have through grace that they were prepared to meet Him. And let us labor and pray that we may also be ready, for our Lord has warned us that He will come at an hour we do not expect (Matthew 24:44).

I close with the Apostle Paul's exhortation: "Therefore, my beloved brethren, be ye steadfast, unmovable, always abounding in the work of the Lord, forasmuch as ye know that your labor is not in vain in the Lord," (1 Corinthians 15:58).

May each of us demonstrate the same diligence toward the full assurance of our hope unto the end (Hebrews 6:11).

Other Books on Heresy at Puritan Publications

The Growth and Spreading of Heresy by Thomas Hodges (1600-1672)
How does heresy invade Christ's church, and grow? Thomas Hodges shows how heresy grows and spreads, and what Christians can do to guard against it in this rare puritan work.

The Works of Henry Greenwood by Henry Greenwood (1545-1634)
While there are many ways in the world, only the way of godliness, Christianity, and the Word of God, leads to eternal life. See how Greenwood explains this throughout this compilation of his works.

A Brief Description of Heretics by Ephraim Pagitt (1575-1647)
Heresy in the church is exceedingly destructive. This work is a wonderful *summation* of many of the heresies that have plagued the church throughout history, as well as in our own day. Added to this work is also Obadiah Sedgwick's sermon on "The Nature and Danger of Heresies."

The Reformation's Light by John Calvin, *et al*
The writings of the Reformers themselves hold the marrow and the blessing of the Reformation. In this little volume are a series of encouraging writings written by four Reformation giants Beza, Latimer, Calvin and Knox. Awesome faith-building writings.

Historical Theology Made Easy by C. Matthew McMahon
Everyone needs to understand where their beliefs came from in the history of the church. This work in the "made easy" series, covers all you need to know about Historical Theology in an easy to understand format!

The False Teacher Tried and Cast by John Brinsley (1600-1665)
False teachers abound throughout church history. Today they are more prevalent than ever. Brinsley helps us make note of what a false teacher is, and how to try teachers to see if they are true or false. This is an important work for our day and age.

An Antidote Against Blasphemy by John Brinsley (1600-1665)
Do you blaspheme? It is easy to see heathen blaspheme God. But what about Christians? And what is the antidote to blasphemy? John Brinsley's masterful treatise was encouraged to be read by both Simeon Ashe and Edmund Calamy (Westminster puritans). It is definitely a book for us today.

www.ingramcontent.com/pod-product-compliance
Lightning Source LLC
Chambersburg PA
CBHW020332170426
43200CB00006B/355